# STRANGE
## BUT TRUE

WRITTEN BY **KATHRYN HULICK**

ILLUSTRATED BY **GORDY WRIGHT**

Frances Lincoln
Children's Books

# INTRODUCTION

Ghosts. Aliens. Lost cities. Mind-reading powers. Sea monsters. These are some of the many mysteries that await in the pages of this book. Some of these stories will intrigue and beguile you. At first, they may seem very convincing. But keep your wits sharp. Question everything. Our challenge for you is to discover the truth.

To do this, the best tool you have at your disposal is science. Science is not a system of rules or beliefs. It is a method that people use to better understand the world. Scientists are naturally curious and full of wonder. So they work to solve mysteries, replacing ignorance with knowledge. Basically, the scientific method works like this: gather evidence, study the evidence, and come up with a hypothesis, or an idea, that could explain the evidence.

The next step is to test your hypothesis. You might be tempted to try to prove it right. Many people search only for evidence to support their beliefs. For example, some Bigfoot hunters claim every knocking sound in the forest is the beast they seek. But this is bad science. The best way to find out whether a hypothesis is a strong idea is to try to prove it wrong. You have to put your desires and beliefs aside and focus only on the evidence.

If you can't investigate a mystery in person, at the place or time it occurred, then you have to rely on what others have said about it. The closer a source is to the original event, the more accurate the information should be. Also watch out for events that seem to be

related, but may not be. For example, perhaps an archaeologist died just after digging up an ancient mummy. Did the mummy cause the death? It's easy to jump to this conclusion. But you need more evidence to prove that it isn't just a coincidence.

In any mystery, the most likely explanation is the one that makes the fewest assumptions. This is a principle called Occam's Razor. Did a ghost scratch at the window, or a tree branch? Even if you have zero evidence either way, you know that tree branches exist. Explanations involving natural, well-understood forces are always more likely to be true than ones involving supernatural or unknown forces.

So when you're reading about each mystery, check the sources. Interrogate the evidence. Watch out for coincidences. And remember that simple explanations are more likely to be true. At the same time, keep an open mind. A hypothesis may seem too strange to be true. But evidence could always prove it to be correct. You should not dismiss an idea until you have carefully considered it.

Feel free to enjoy these mysteries. Feel free to dream about the possibilities of forces and beings beyond those known to science. An active imagination leads to insightful ideas. But you must also practice the art of doubt. If you do this, you might just discover which mysteries are truly unsolved and which fantastic ideas could really be true.

# CONTENTS

# AN ENCOUNTER WITH ALIENS

*A car drives along an empty stretch of highway late one night in the mountains of New Hampshire, USA. Out of nowhere, a bright light appears. Could it be a falling star?*

*I*t is September 19, 1961, and Betty and Barney Hill are on their way home from vacation in Montréal, Canada. Strangely, the bright light seems to follow them. Then the car starts to vibrate and the Hills hear strange buzzing and beeping sounds. A feeling of drowsiness washes over them.

Suddenly, they find themselves 35 miles further south. They have vague memories of taking a sudden turn and encountering a roadblock. But several hours have passed that they cannot explain. They arrive home around dawn. When they get there, they discover that Barney's binocular strap is broken and his shoes are scuffed. Betty later notices that her dress is torn and stained.

*A few years later, under hypnosis, the Hills recall a horrifying ordeal.*

Ten days later, Betty starts having vivid dreams about going through an alien abduction. A few years later, under hypnosis, the Hills recall a horrifying ordeal. In this memory, the light drops rapidly and a large, disc-shaped ship hovers overhead. Barney gets out and peers through his binoculars at an astonishing sight. Almost a dozen figures in black uniforms stare out from inside the craft. The figures, who look like humans, take Barney and Betty inside. They bring them to different rooms and put each of them through a series of medical tests and procedures. Betty cries out when her examiner pierces her belly button with a sharp needle. But then she talks to her captors. They show

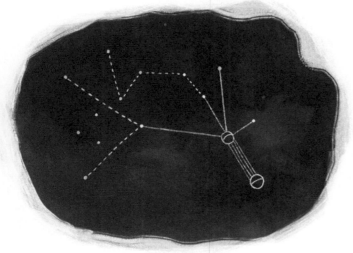

her a book full of strange symbols and a map of stars. After one of the hypnosis sessions, Betty draws the star map her captors showed her. The map seems to represent the Zeta Reticuli system, a pair of dim stars located around 230 trillion miles from Earth. Could the Hills have been the victims of an alien abduction?

# ✗ THE FIRST FLYING SAUCERS

The Hills' experience became famous. But it wasn't the first—or last—alien encounter to capture the public's imagination. Many people have seen lights or flying objects that they can't explain. In June 1947, pilot Kenneth Arnold was flying near Mount Rainier in Washington state when he saw nine objects flying in formation along the ridgeline of the mountains. He described them as looking like saucers skipping across water. The name "flying saucer" stuck, and the news of this sighting spread around the world.

A few weeks later, a rancher named Mack Brazel brought some unusual debris to the sheriff of Roswell, New Mexico: tinfoil, rubber, and pieces of a strangely lightweight—yet strong—reflective material. Brazel had found the stuff scattered on his property, and wondered if it could be the wreckage of a flying saucer. The nearby Roswell Army Air Force Base had no idea what to make of the debris, either. They told the media that they had recovered a flying disc. Shortly afterwards, higher-up government officials claimed it was just a crashed weather balloon. But those who had seen weather balloons before didn't believe it. Was this a government conspiracy to cover up a real alien landing?

*Was this a government conspiracy to cover up a real alien landing?*

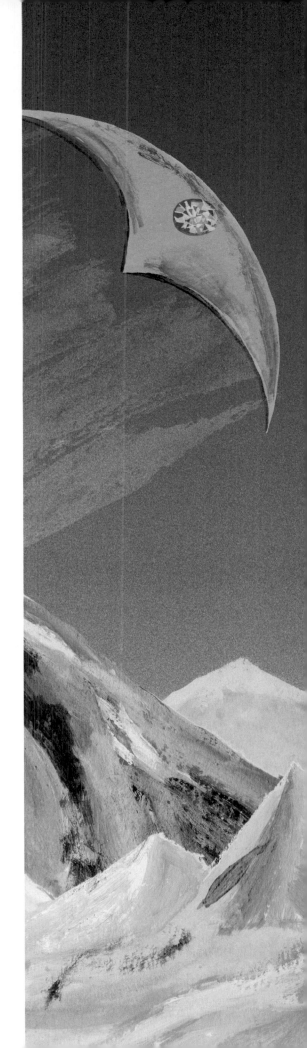

Soon after these two incidents, sightings of flying saucers began flooding in from all over the United States. In 1952, the Air Force launched Project Blue Book to investigate what they dubbed UFOs, short for "unidentified flying objects." Though this investigation ended, sightings have continued.

Today, the Mutual UFO Network (MUFON) logs over 500 reports every month of sightings from around the world. Could all of these people, including the Hills, be wrong?

## ✗ PROBLEMS WITH PERCEPTION

In many cases, people really do see strange lights or shapes in the sky. But that doesn't mean extraterrestrials have visited Earth. There are other, more rational explanations. For example, the crashed craft at Roswell was actually a top-secret US government attempt to spy on the Soviet Union during the Cold War. It was a balloon carrying a sensing device complete with microphones and a disc-shaped antenna. Most of the officials who looked at the debris knew nothing about the new technology, so wrongly assumed that it wasn't human.

Human technology and natural events get mistaken for UFOs all the time. Common false alarms include stars, planets, unusual clouds, mirages, flares, balloons, rocket launches, drones, and more. How do people mistake these things for alien spacecraft? It's important to understand that what you see is not always actually what's out there in the world. "It's a recreation in your brain of what you think you're seeing," explains James McGaha, a retired US Air Force major and an astronomer.

The brain is a machine that works to keep you safe. When early humans had to watch out for dangerous animals, it was safer to believe that a rustling sound or shadow was a beast than to assume it was the wind or a trick of the light. The brain seeks edges, shapes, patterns, and connections. It often finds things that could be considered a threat—like alien aircraft—even when they aren't really there. For example, the objects that Arnold saw were probably a mirage, says McGaha. Mirages are illusions that happen when light bends as it passes through layers of cold and warm air.

*Many people living in and around Phoenix, Arizona saw a triangular pattern of lights in the sky.*

In March 1997, many people living in and around Phoenix, Arizona saw a triangular pattern of lights in the sky. An amateur astronomer watching the sky that night through a telescope identified the lights as airplanes. However, some witnesses were adamant that the lights were all part of one huge spacecraft. Perhaps their brains filled in the space between the lights to make a larger shape. Videos showed the lights changing position from a V-shape to a straight line, something that lights on a single craft would not do.

So what about the Hills? They most likely really d d see a strange light in the sky, too. Jim Macdonald, a resident of the area in which the Hills claimed to be abducted, thinks the light was actually an ordinary light on top of Cannon Mountain.  He's seen it many times driving that same route. Perhaps he is right. However, if the 'spaceship' Betty and Barney saw was really just a light, how is it possible that they remember going on board?

✘

## DREAMS VS REALITY

The Hills aren't alone in believing that they've had contact with aliens. Today, people who have seen or encountered extraterrestrials call themselves Experiencers. Some report scary or terrifying abductions. But many others feel special or lucky to have come into contact with otherworldly beings. They often believe that extraterrestrials are here to help humanity. They are likely not lying about what they saw, heard, or felt  But that doesn't mean alien encounters actually happened.

Personal experiences aren't always accurate. For example, in a hallucination, a fully awake person experiences sights, sounds, tastes, or textures that aren't really there. They might feel real, but they aren't. This is very rare, and usually indicates a mental illness or other health disorder. However, at night, in dreams, we all experience vivid events that are completely imaginary. When we wake up, if we even remember any dreams, we realize that they were not real. But right at the edge between wakefulness and sleep, reality blurs. This is called the hypnagogic state. While just falling asleep or just waking up, or in a dreamy state such as hypnosis or meditation, a completely healthy person may experience some truly bizarre things.

*In dreams, we all experience vivid events that are completely imaginary.*

*Right at the edge between wakefulness and sleep, reality blurs.*

One of those strange experiences is called sleep paralysis. During sleep, the brain prevents the rest of the body from moving. This keeps you from thrashing around and hurting yourself while dreaming. But sometimes, a person starts to wake up while still in this paralyzed state. The person usually sees his or her real surroundings, but sights, sounds, and other sensations leak in from the dream state. Often, it seems as if someone else is in the room. At the same time, it's impossible to move, speak, or breathe deeply.

*Sometimes, a person starts to wake up while still in this paralyzed state.*

Psychologist Susan Clancy spent several years interviewing people who say they've encountered aliens. Some of their stories sounded exactly like sleep paralysis. A computer programmer she calls Mike said, "I woke up around 3 AM and couldn't move. I managed to open my eyes and there were creatures in the room with me. I saw shadowy figures around my bed..." And another man, a dermatologist she calls James, said, "I found myself waking up in the middle of the night, seized with fear. There were beings standing around my bed, but I was totally paralyzed, incapable of moving."

*'There were beings standing around my bed, but I was totally paralyzed, incapable of moving.'*

# FALSE MEMORIES

Sleep paralysis helps explain some instances of encounters with aliens. But not all. Betty and Barney Hill weren't in bed or paralyzed when they saw a strange light. In their case and in many other cases of alien encounters, the complete story of what happened only emerged after hypnosis. During the 1980s and 1990s, many professional psychotherapists believed that hypnosis was a good tool to bring back lost or forgotten memories. But since then, experts have come to realize that hypnosis can actually create false memories. How is this possible?

*Many people think that memory is like a video recording of an event. But unlike a video, a memory does not remain the same every time you think about it.*

Many people think that memory is like a video recording of an event. But unlike a video, a memory does not remain the same every time you think about it. Every time you remember something, the brain rebuilds the memory, often with new details. If someone suggests that something happened to you, even if it didn't, you may begin to remember it happening. When this suggestion happens before or during hypnosis, the mind may create a fantasy that feels like a vivid, real memory.

A person won't create a memory about an alien abduction out of nowhere. Clancy found that the people she interviewed all believed in aliens before remembering an encounter with them. Betty was interested in UFOs long before the sighting. Also, it's important to remember that she dreamt about an alien abduction shortly after the event. Her dreams, which she almost definitely shared with her husband, included all the main events which she later 'remembered' through hypnosis. Could Betty and Barney have just been remembering Betty's dreams, rather than the reality of what happened that night?

Television may have also played a part. At first, Betty described the aliens as short men with black hair and big noses. But she changed her story after hearing one of Barney's hypnosis sessions. He remembered the aliens with gray skin, huge eyes, and large, bald heads. This matched the alien character in an episode of the TV show *Outer Limits* that had aired less than two weeks earlier. Many years later, Barney claimed never to have seen the show. However, it's an uncanny coincidence. Perhaps he forgot about watching it, or saw advertisements for it.

But what about the map Betty drew? An amateur astronomer named Marjorie Fish painstakingly searched until she found that it matched the Zeta Reticuli system. But she based her search on information from 1969. A later survey of the sky revealed the map didn't match after all.

# ✗ UNEXPLAINED . . . BUT NOT UNEXPLAINABLE

So what really happened to the Hills that night? Something certainly made their journey take longer than expected. It was late at night and they'd been driving for a very long time. They remembered feeling drowsy, a common sign of a state of reduced awareness called "highway hypnosis."

*Something certainly made their journey take longer than expected.*

Perhaps they drifted off the road or took a wrong turn, and got out of the car while trying to figure out what happened. This could help explain the reported damage to the shoes, binocular strap, and dress. A disturbing event like this, coupled with Betty's interest in UFOs, may have inspired her to dream about an alien abduction. She shared her dreams with her husband and later these were recalled and new details added under hypnosis, which made the dreams feel like real memories. We'll never know for sure, but perhaps this is the most likely explanation.

*A lack of information may make it impossible to identify the real cause of a strange light.*

The truth is that there are many UFO and alien encounter stories which aren't easily explained away. Believers like to offer unexplained sightings as evidence that something otherworldly must be happening. But "unexplained" does not imply "unexplainable." A lack of information may make it impossible to identify the real cause of a strange light. Casual observers often don't note the time, date, location, distance, speed, duration, or other facts which could solve the mystery.

And in very rare cases, a strange light remains mysterious even after some serious analysis. In the remote valley of Hessdalen in Norway, balls of lights have been appearing, hovering, and flashing regularly since the 1980s. Some UFO enthusiasts have claimed the valley is a portal to other worlds. And some skeptics say it's all a hoax.

Meanwhile, a small group of scientists has been methodically measuring the lights and collecting data since 1983. One of their theories suggests that the valley may act as a giant natural battery. The rocks on one side of the river contain copper and those on the other side contain iron and zinc. And sulfur from an abandoned mine flows through a river at the bottom of the valley. This unique arrangement may produce an electric field. But the field on its own wouldn't make visible light. It needs another energy source. This may come from the sun. When its activity increases, it pelts Earth with bursts of radiation. Sometimes, the scientists suspect, this may spark lights in the valley.

The source of the Hessdalen lights remains a mystery. But extraterrestrial visitors are a very unlikely explanation. The truth is that the natural world is an amazing place that we still don't fully understand.

## ✗ REAL ALIENS

*"We are beginning our own exploration of space, so it's entirely reasonable there would be others who have done so."*

Someday, people may encounter alien life. It's not impossible. "We are beginning our own exploration of space, so it's entirely reasonable there would be others who have done so," says James Oberg, a retired NASA engineer. Since life evolved on Earth, the same process could certainly take place elsewhere in the universe. It's a huge place. "There are billions and billions of galaxies, each one with about 200 billion stars like our Sun," says Eddie Irizarry, a solar system ambassador for NASA. Planets circle some of those stars. And some of those planets may have the right conditions for life.

However, to arrive at Earth, an alien species would need to develop enough intelligence to build technology more advanced than our own. Plus, they would then need to explore far beyond their home planet and discover Earth. So most astrophysicists are not expecting to encounter intelligent life any time soon. Rather, they focus on looking for planets with the conditions to support any kind of life.

One of the most important ingredients for life as we know it is liquid water. In our own solar system, liquid water lurks beneath ice caps on moons of Jupiter and Saturn as well as on Mars. If life does thrive in these hidden waters, it is most likely microscopic. Bacteria and other microbes can survive in extreme conditions on Earth. So it's reasonable to expect that they are much more common in the universe than more complex life forms like us. Perhaps one day, we will be the aliens who visit another planet and abduct its microbial life.

# THE HAUNTED MANSION

*The Monte Cristo Homestead was once grand and new. But it has fallen into ruin after decades of neglect. Vandals stripped lead from the roof and broke all the windows. Squatters pulled up floorboards and burned them in the fireplace.*

In 1963, Olive and Reginald Ryan purchase the run-down mansion in Junee, Australia and begin to repair it. Late one evening, after a shopping trip to pick up building supplies, they return home to an astonishing sight. Bright light streams from every door and window. That seems impossible. The house has no electricity! The Ryans think burglars are inside. Or maybe squatters returned. They tell their kids to stay in the car. Then, as they approach to investigate, the lights vanish. They find no one inside.

This is only the first of many unnerving experiences for the Ryans and their five children. They regularly hear footsteps walking across an upstairs balcony, and sometimes see a woman in white standing there. Olive feels hands resting on her shoulders when no one is there. Reginald hangs a picture, then finds it fallen on the floor but unbroken, two nights in a row. And in the most disturbing incident of all, one evening one of their daughters goes to check on her sleeping little brother, and

*They regularly hear footsteps walking across an upstairs balcony.*

sees an elderly man in old-fashioned clothes standing at the end of his bed. She races off, screaming to her family about a man in the house. But they find no one. The little brother, Lawrence Ryan, learns about this incident as a teenager, then moves out of the main house to a different bedroom. He says, "I always felt like someone was watching me in that room." Was that someone a ghost?

Christopher William Crawley, the wealthy and powerful founder of the town of Junee, once lived in the mansion with his wife, children, and numerous servants. The family hosted fancy balls and played tennis and golf on the grounds. Crawley died in the home at the age of 69 after a boil on his neck got infected. After his death, the locals say, his wife almost never left the house. She died there at the age of 92.

*"I always felt like someone was watching me in that room."*

But the property's creepy history began long before their deaths. According to local lore, a young maid fell from the balcony to her death. She was rumored to be pregnant at the time, and some believe she was killed to cover up that fact. Could she be the source of the footsteps and female figure on the balcony? Another servant, a stableboy, supposedly suffered lethal burns when his straw mattress was set on fire. The Crawleys' youngest child, a baby daughter named Magdalena, died in a fall down the stairs. Some think her nanny may have dropped her on purpose. Could the spirits of all of these people still haunt the place where they died?

# A MENAGERIE OF SPIRITS

If you believe in ghosts, you're not alone. A 2017 poll found that around half of Americans believe that places can be haunted by spirits. Polls in many other countries around the world produce similar results. Belief in ghosts depends on what you think happens after death. The physical body perishes, but what happens to your consciousness? Are you gone forever? Or do you continue to experience this world or another world in some way? Many people believe in a soul or something similar that survives past death. It's not a huge step from the idea of an afterlife to the belief that spirits may influence the world of the living. However, people from different cultures tell very different stories about how and why ghosts appear.

*Many people believe in a soul or something similar that survives past death.*

In ancient Mesopotamia, people believed that sickness was a punishment inflicted by spirits of the dead. In Mexico and parts of Central America, everyone knows the legend of La Llorona, the weeping woman. In one version of the story, she drowned her own children, and now haunts riverbanks, calling and crying for them. In China and parts of Southeast Asia today, many people ask the spirits of their ancestors for blessings. During the Hungry Ghost Festival, people in this region burn paper or incense and leave out gifts, food, tea, and sweets. They believe that these offerings will please the ghosts and help prevent bad luck.

Ghost stories can be fascinating, scary, and memorable. But they are just stories. Only physical evidence could show that ghosts are real. People who call themselves ghost hunters or paranormal investigators search for this evidence. Some claim to have found it.

# HUNTING FOR PHANTOMS

Ghost hunters often arm themselves with a variety of high-tech equipment, including cameras and audio recorders as well as instruments that measure temperature (ghosts supposedly create cold spots) or detect motion. Electromagnetic field (EMF) meters are especially popular. Electromagnetic energy comes in a wide spectrum that includes everything from high-energy X-rays to low-energy radio waves. Visible light falls in the middle of the spectrum. Electricians use EMF meters to detect the energy that electrical wires and devices emit, which is in the radio frequency range. This energy is strongest right next to the source, but weakens rapidly with distance. When EMF readers detect fluctuations, or rising and falling amounts of electromagnetic energy, some think this indicates a ghostly presence.

*Cameras may capture still images or videos that show shadowy figures, glowing wisps, or orbs of light.*

*Audio equipment may record what seem to be faint voices saying short phrases, like "Get out."*

Investigators set up their equipment in a haunted location and wait. Often, they find nothing. But occasionally, they record something unusual. Cameras may capture still images or videos that show shadowy figures, glowing wisps, or orbs of light. Audio equipment may record what seem to be faint voices saying short phrases, like "Get out." This is called Electronic Voice Phenomenon, or EVP for short. An EMF meter may fluctuate wildly, indicating a source of energy. These recordings seem intriguing. But are they really evidence of ghosts?

# SPOOKY FACES AND MURMURING VOICES

Photos and audio anomalies may seem like convincing evidence. But it's a mistake to jump directly to a supernatural explanation for a strange photo or recording. First, you have to consider all possible practical explanations. Remember the principle of Occam's Razor? Simple explanations that make the fewest possible assumptions are always the most likely to be true. When it comes to photographs, many things other than ghosts can explain haunting images.

In the 1860s, photographer William H. Mumler captured images that seemed to show deceased relatives hovering over living family members. His most famous image shows a ghostly Abraham Lincoln with his hands on the shoulders of his widow, Mary Todd Lincoln. The photo was taken a few years after the American president's assassination.

*Many people believed that the dead could communicate with the living.*

During the mid to late 19th century in America, many people who called themselves spiritualists believed that the dead could communicate with the living. Special ceremonies called seances were held in an attempt to talk to the dead. People also used ouija boards, which look like game boards covered in letters and numbers, to channel what seemed to be messages from spirits. Spiritualists believed that Mumler's photos were the real deal, but others accused him of fraud. In very early cameras, a sensitive glass plate captured the image. If this plate was not cleaned well enough, a faint image from a previous photograph might show up in the background of a new photo. Mumler later admitted that one of his first ghost photos happened accidentally when he forgot to clean a plate. Others were likely deliberate hoaxes.

Many modern ghost images are also the result of mistakes, technical glitches, or deliberate hoaxes. If a person moves quickly past a camera while a photo is being taken, for example, the image may show a blurry streak. Flash photographs often capture mysterious orbs of light. Some call these spirit energy. More likely, the flash reflected off of dust or water droplets on or near the lens.

Some ghost images are not technical glitches but psychological ones. For example, a photo from the Monte Cristo homestead seems to show the baby Magdalena's face in a mirror. Most likely, it is not a face at all, but a random reflection that happens to resemble a face. To experience this for yourself, take a look at the moon the next time it's full. Do you see a face? Many people do. People also regularly see familiar shapes in clouds. This phenomenon is called pareidolia. It happens because it's very important for the brain to identify familiar patterns, like faces. So sometimes the brain finds faces where there are none.

*So sometimes the brain finds faces where there are none.*

Similarly, the brain may find words in static or random noise. This is the most likely explanation in many examples of EVP. In other cases, the audio equipment may have captured distant voices or music that were too faint for human ears to hear. Ghost hunting teaches the important lesson that using technical equipment does not make an investigation scientific.

29

Anomalies in data only seem like evidence of ghosts because that's what ghost hunters are looking for. Noah Leigh has led the Paranormal Investigators of Milwaukee group for over ten years. When his group hunts for EVPs, they ask a question, then leave ten seconds of silence to allow for an answer. They use strict procedures to help rule out noise from growling stomachs, squeaky doors, and other background sounds. He says, "In all our years doing this, we've never had a direct response to a question, ever."

✗

# HOW TO HAUNT A HOUSE

*In some people, these vibrations may cause feelings of uneasiness or fear.*

If a haunted location isn't really home to wandering spirits of the dead, then why do so many people have strange experiences at a place like the Monte Cristo Homestead? What makes a house haunted? Scientists have proposed some intriguing theories. Some blame infrasound. These sounds are too low to hear, but the body feels their vibrations. In some people, these vibrations may cause feelings of uneasiness or fear. Others have studied how electromagnetic fields affect the brain. In people with a certain form of epilepsy, a part of the brain called the temporal lobe malfunctions, causing visions that are often religious in nature. Some scientists have studied whether electromagnetic fields might trigger this same effect in people without epilepsy. The fields may come from natural sources, such as minor earthquakes or tremors. Or they might come from power lines, cell phones, appliances, and other devices.

However, experimentation has shed doubt on these theories. In 2004, psychologist Christopher French and his colleagues at Goldsmiths University of London attempted to create a haunted room. They set up and hid devices that would generate electromagnetic fields and infrasound. One by one, seventy-nine volunteers entered the room, a cool, dimly lit, empty, white, circular space, and stayed there for fifty minutes. The researchers told the volunteers they might have some unusual sensations and asked them to record any such experiences. Some volunteers got bombarded with electromagnetic fields and infrasound, others with one or the other, and a control group with nothing. But it didn't matter which group a volunteer was in. People in the control group were just as likely to report weird sensations as people in the other groups. What was going on?

*The researchers told the volunteers they might have some unusual sensations and asked them to record any such experiences.*

After everyone left the room, they all completed a personality test. Suggestible people—those who easily accept what others tell them to do or believe—tend to get high scores on a certain part of the test. Everyone who reported strange experiences also got high scores on this part of the test. So they seem to have experienced strange things in the room not because of energy fields or vibrations, but because the researchers told them they would. In other words, people experience strange things in haunted houses because they're expecting strange things to happen.

Alternately, someone who experiences strange things may turn to ghosts as a fitting explanation. This is similar to what happens in many alien and UFO experiences. The things people see are created in the brain and do not always represent reality. A hallucination, vivid dream, or even a trick of the light may seem like a real encounter with a ghost.

# REAL WORLD EXPERIENCE

So what about the Monte Cristo Homestead? Today, Lawrence Ryan leads ghost tours there. But we may never know what really happened in the haunted mansion. Some of the tragic deaths may not actually have occurred, or may not have been murders. It's often impossible to go back and find out the truth about events that happened many years ago. Even if murders did occur, these stories likely only serve to make visitors more uneasy and primed for unusual experiences.

Joe Nickell is a detective who has spent his entire career looking for realistic explanations for events that seem paranormal. "It doesn't matter what you and I believe," he says. "It matters what we have evidence for." He has investigated many reportedly haunted places. In one of his first cases, he discovered that the footsteps people heard on a haunted staircase came from a very real iron staircase located in the building next door. Similarly, the strange light inside the Monte Cristo homestead could have come from people in the house, just as the Ryans first suspected. If squatters were in the house, they likely knew they weren't supposed to be there and fled when they saw the car. Just because the Ryans never figured out a real-world source of the light, the footsteps, the figure on the balcony, the man in the bedroom, or other strange events does not mean that there wasn't one.

*"If you come to our place you can make up your own mind."*

Lawrence Ryan is inclined to believe in ghosts after his experience growing up at the Monte Cristo Homestead. But he doesn't push anything on his guests. "If you come to our place you can make up your own mind," he says.

# THE SEARCH FOR LOST WORLDS

*A palace adorned with gold, silver, and ivory rises above an island in the middle of the Atlantic Ocean. Here, natural fountains spew out both hot and cold water, feeding luxurious baths as well as all manner of trees, flowers and fruits.*

Strips of sea water separate the central island from two more bands of land. Bridges and aqueducts join the concentric circles together into one city, and a massive wall surrounds the entire metropolis. A race-course for horses runs all around the widest band of land. In a busy harbor outside the wall, ships and merchants arrive from all over the world.

This mighty city is Atlantis. The year is around 9300 BCE. The people of the city descend directly from Poseidon, the Greek god of the sea. At first, Atlanteans were noble and good. But over time, they have become greedy and power-hungry. They've established a mighty empire that extends as far as Egypt. And now they are at war with ancient Athens. This angers Zeus, king of the gods. The Atlanteans have to be punished.

*In a single day and night, the entire island disappears into the sea.*

As the unsuspecting citizens go about their business, the gods strike. Buildings and bridges topple as earthquakes rock the land. Floods drown the gardens and baths. In a single day and night, the entire island disappears into the depths of the sea.

The Greek philosopher Plato introduced the story of Atlantis during the 300s BCE, over two thousand years ago. In Plato's writings, the teacher Socrates asks a student for an example of how a perfect society has succeeded during a time of struggle. The student then tells the story above of ancient Athens and the city called Atlantis. He begins, "Then listen, Socrates, to a tale which though strange, is certainly true…"

But is the story really true? Over the years, countless scholars and explorers have tried to find the lost city of Atlantis, but none of them have quite proved successful. So where is the lost city, if it even exists?

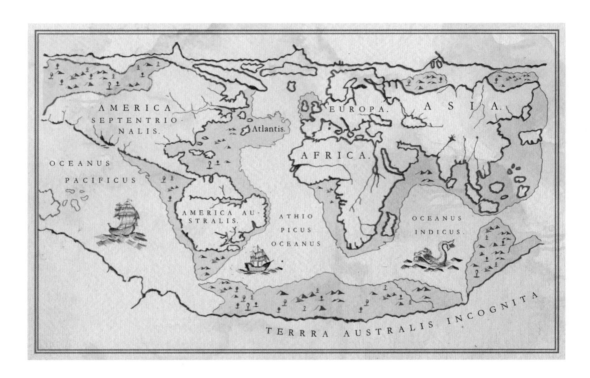

## A NEW WORLD

*Over the years, countless scholars and explorers have tried to find the lost city of Atlantis.*

Plato's story was relatively unknown until the Renaissance in Europe. When European explorers arrived in the New World in the 16th century, interest in Atlantis surged. The Spanish historian Francisco López de Gómara suggested that the Aztecs—a civilization living in Mexico—might have been refugees from Atlantis.

He cited as evidence the fact that in the Aztec language, the word *atl* means water. One scholar even made a map of where he thought Atlantis had been.

In the 1800s, the story of the city that fell into the sea grew and changed. Madame Helena Blavatsky taught that humans evolved from astral jellyfish into four-armed, egg-laying creatures that lived on a lost Pacific island civilization called Lemuria or Mu. In a later stage of evolution, she said, giant humans lived on Atlantis. A lot of what Helena Blavatsky said seems quite ridiculous, especially given what we now know about human evolution. But her contemporary, US congressman Ignatius Donnelly, wrote a book that persuaded many people that Atlantis had to be real. He theorized that Atlantis was the source of all human civilization. William Ewart Gladstone, the prime minister of Britain at the time, wrote a long letter to Donnelly saying, "I am much disposed to believe in Atlantis." Was Donnelly right?

*He theorized that Atlantis was the source of all human civilization.*

If he was, it would be an incredible discovery. In 9300 BCE, sabre-toothed cats, woolly rhinoceroses and giant cave bears still roamed the Earth. Humans, according to archaeological evidence, had not advanced beyond the hunter-gatherer stage. Could an advanced civilization really have existed so long ago? In the next century, something happened which seemed to prove it.

# THE SLEEPING PROPHET

*He claimed that Atlantis had power plants, flying boats, and other fantastic technologies.*

In 1933, a man named Edgar Cayce slipped into a trance. He soon began to speak in vivid detail about the technology of the city of Atlantis. Cayce, also known as "The Sleeping Prophet," first became famous in the 1920s for his psychic abilities. He could supposedly diagnose illnesses and offer cures while in a sleep-like state. In various trances, he claimed that Atlantis had power plants, flying boats, and other fantastic technologies. He also helped some people explore their past lives as citizens of Atlantis.

In that 1933 session, he said, "In the sunken portions of Atlantis, or Poseidia, a portion of the temples may yet be discovered, under the slime of ages of sea water, near what is known as Bimini, off the coast of Florida." And in 1940, he predicted a date for this discovery. "And Poseidia will be among the first portions of Atlantis to rise again. Expect it in sixty-eight and sixty-nine; not so far away!"

In 1968, the year that Edgar Cayce had predicted, three divers exploring off the coast of Bimini came upon an amazing sight. A path formed from flat, rectangular blocks of stone stretched off into the distance for around 1600 feet. The path was perfectly straight except for a J-shaped curve at one end. Several shorter paths ran parallel to this one. Delicate sea fans and barnacles clung to the stones, which had clearly eroded and rounded with age. But the straight edges and even corners made the blocks seem out of place and unnatural. Could it be an ancient road?

*In several spots, they found cement and marble columns on the sea floor.*

*Had the lost city of Atlantis finally been discovered?*

The next year, the divers returned with a pair of pilots willing to fly over the area in search of more evidence. From the air, the pilots saw structures on the sea floor that turned out to be cement and marble columns. A media frenzy followed. Had the lost city of Atlantis finally been discovered?

# A NATURAL PHENOMENON

'At first sight you would guess it was put there by humans.'

The fact that the discovery of the Bimini Road and the columns occurred in the exact year Cayce had predicted was enough to convince a lot of people. However, when you look closely at the facts, Cayce's prophecy no longer seems so magical. Atlantis didn't actually "rise again" in 1968 and 1969 as he predicted. And if the site really were home to an ancient civilization, then divers should have found human artifacts. All they found were the columns, which all likely came from shipwrecks. Plus, many experts argue that the Bimini road is simply an incredible—and natural—phenomenon.

Eugene Shinn, a retired geologist, understands why people got so excited about the Bimini road. "At first sight you would guess it was put there by humans," he says. But he also understands a lot about how rocks form in the ocean. On many beaches, as waves batter the sand, a mineral called aragonite fills in the spaces between grains just below the beach. Over time, this mineral effectively glues the sand grains together like cement, forming beachrock. In many places, beachrock remains hidden beneath a sandy layer on top of the beach. But on Bimini and several other places, erosion washes the loose sand away, leaving beach rock exposed in a long line along the beach. The sun then heats and cracks the rock, often in very straight lines. Cement sidewalks crack in a very similar way. Over time, this path of beach rock can end up submerged under the ocean just off the shore, looking very much like an ancient road.

In the 1970s, Shinn's team took samples from several of the rocks. A lab at the University of Miami used carbon dating to determine that the sand grains inside the rocks were 2,000 to 3,000 years old. "That was about the time that Plato was living," says Shinn. Atlantis was supposedly destroyed 9,300 years ago. The sand grains that formed the rocks did not even exist back then. It also turned out that one of the divers who found the Bimini road, Joseph Manson Valentine, was a huge fan of Edgar Cayce. He may have intentionally set out to find evidence of Atlantis near Bimini in 1968 because he believed in Cayce's prophecy. Since he was expecting to find something amazing, he did.

Atlantis supposedly sunk 9,300 years earlier. The sand grains that formed the rocks did not even exist back then.

# THE SEARCH CONTINUES

If Atlantis isn't near Bimini, then could it be somewhere else? Plato's works say it was an island in the Atlantic Ocean until it sunk and disappeared, but geologists know this to be impossible. How do they know? They have figured out that the Earth's crust is made up of large, interlocking pieces, called plates. These plates move, or drift, very slowly over time. At some edges, old land crashes together and some sinks down—this is the source of most large earthquakes. At other edges, new land or sea floor forms as molten rock pushes upward. In the Atlantic Ocean, the second process has been going on for millions of years, since long before Atlantis was supposed to have existed. New sea floor

*Plato's works say it was an island in the Atlantic Ocean until it sunk and disappeared, but geologists know this to be impossible.*

has been forming and spreading, enlarging the ocean gradually over time. Plato described Atlantis as "larger than Libya and Asia put together." It's just not possible that a landmass that huge sank down and disappeared, given what geologists know about the movement of Earth's plates.

*One of the most popular theories suggests that real events at the Mediterranean islands of Crete and Thera inspired the Atlantis story.*

However, what if Atlantis wasn't in the Atlantic Ocean at all? Some people think that Plato could have been writing about—or at least inspired by—different locations. One of the most popular theories suggests that real events on the Mediterranean islands of Crete and Thera (now called Santorini) inspired the Atlantis story.

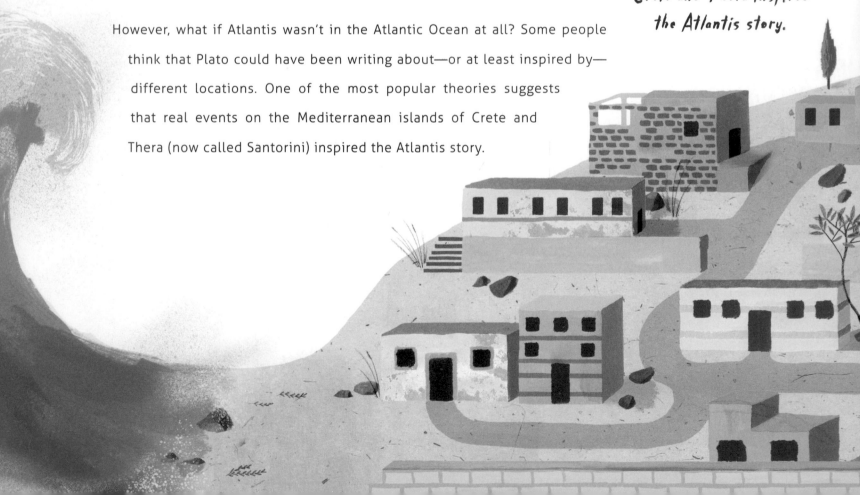

Crete was once home to the advanced Minoan civilization. Like the Atlanteans, they built splendid palaces. They also had paved roads and a written language.

In 1500 BCE, a huge volcanic eruption tore apart the island of Thera, possibly dumping chunks of the island into the sea and sending massive waves towards Crete. Within fifty years of the disaster, the Minoan civilization was no more. It's a fascinating tale of a real civilization defeated by the sea, and there's a chance these events may have inspired Plato. However, a key aspect of Plato's story was the war between Atlantis and Athens, which is missing entirely. Plus, Atlantis was supposed to have fallen into the sea thousands of years before the volcanic eruption on Thera.

In 2017, a documentary team including James Cameron, a famous film director, attempted to find Atlantis. Plato wrote that the island was located in the Atlantic Ocean, beyond the "Pillars of Hercules." Most scholars identify those as the Strait of Gibraltar, a narrow band of sea separating Spain from Morocco. On the Atlantic side of the strait, the team discovered ancient anchors. Though a fascinating find, the anchors are likely from the Bronze Age, which is at least 7,000 years later than the date Plato said Atlantis existed.

Many other locations have been suggested as Atlantis, including the Sahara Desert, Greenland, Iceland, Zimbabwe, Indonesia, and even Antarctica, but—for a number of different reasons—none of them completely fit Plato's account. Most experts therefore agree that the most likely explanation is that Plato invented the story of Atlantis in order to make a point. His works are commonly understood to be fictional stories intended to teach moral lessons. The lesson in this case was that the citizens of Atlantis got too powerful and greedy, so the gods destroyed them.

*The lesson in this case was that the citizens of Atlantis got too powerful and greedy, so the gods destroyed them.*

## ✘ A LOST WORLD DISCOVERED

Atlantis may be just a myth. But could other ancient cities lie beneath the waves, waiting to be discovered? According to a legend from India, the god Krishna established a city of gold in Dwarka in ancient times. After his death, the sea swallowed up the city. Could this legend have some basis in real history? In 1963, divers discovered structures and artifacts underwater off the coast of modern-day Dwarka in Gujarat, India. Some experts believe that a tsunami may have struck the city, causing parts of it to fall into the ocean, which fits with the legend. Modern excavations have uncovered stone anchors and fallen stone structures that may have supported jetties for anchoring boats. An inscription found on one stone block uses a script from the 1500s, but some of the anchors date back as far as 2500 BC. Archaeologists continue to explore the site, attempting to discover its true historical significance.

Many other secrets about ancient people and how they lived remain hidden beneath the ocean and underground. Exploration to discover these secrets is an important part of the science of archaeology. While some continue to hold out hope for Atlantis, serious scientists instead search for more information about ancient cultures that really did exist in India, China, Egypt, the Middle East, South America, and elsewhere. These people built many incredible structures, and some are still waiting to be discovered.

# THE STAR OF DEEP BEGINNING

At the cliff of Bandiagara in Mali, villages perch on high plateaus or nestle at the foot of steep sandstone formations. This has been the home of the Dogon people for several hundred years, and humans have lived in the area for over ten thousand years.

Marcel Griaule, a French anthropologist, arrives in Africa in 1931 to study the Dogon culture. Over a period of several decades, Griaule and his assistants interview elders. The anthropologists record a creation story that reveals a stunning knowledge of astronomy. The Dogon seem to know of Saturn's rings and the existence of four moons around Jupiter.

They also talk of a star of deep beginning that marks the place in the sky where the world was born. This star is invisible but orbits around the brightest star in the sky, Sirius. This turned out to be true. Sirius really does have an invisible twin star, Sirius B, that is too faint to see with the human eye. The Dogon didn't have any telescopes or other astronomical devices. So how did they know these things?

In a creation story that Griaule records, four pairs of twins, fish-like spirits called the Nommo, descend from the heavens in an ark. But what if the arrival of the Nommo isn't just a story? What if it describes the actual landing of an alien spaceship, containing fish-like extraterrestrial visitors that revealed information about the universe to the Dogon? Could this be how they learned about Jupiter, Saturn, and Sirius B?

✗

## THE NAZCA LINES

*Some people argue that there is real, physical proof of an alien visit in the past.*

The Dogon are not the only culture that some believe to have encountered aliens. In fact, some people argue that there is real, physical proof of an alien visit in the past. Over 1,500 years ago, the Nazca, Paracas, and other early human civilizations in Peru and Chile created vast drawings called geoglyphs on flat desert plains. From the air, the designs take shape: a tree, a lizard, a spider. A giant bird stretches out over 985 feet, the length of three football fields placed end to end. Straight lines and geometric shapes also criss-cross the landscape.

Experts know how the figures were made. The Nazca and other cultures moved dark-colored rocks on the surface to the side to reveal the lighter-colored clay beneath. They probably worked from smaller designs to plan the huge drawings, using posts and stretched-out ropes to map out straight lines and curves. The pictures remained intact through the centuries thanks to a lack of wind and rain. But an important question remains: why? The designs reveal themselves most spectacularly when viewed from the air. Yet these ancient people had no flying machines. So what were the lines for?

*The designs reveal themselves most spectacularly when viewed from the air. Yet these ancient people had no flying machines.*

Author Erich Von Däniken asked himself this question. As he flew over the lines, he noticed that the long rectangles next to some of the figures looked a bit like landing strips, like we have today for airplanes. He wondered if the lines and geoglyphs were "signs to beings approaching them from great height." What were those beings? Extraterrestrials. He says the drawings shout, "Land here!" to alien visitors.

# CHARIOTS OF THE GODS

But surely if aliens had visited Earth, historians would have recorded the event? Some people argue that they did. Von Däniken was one of the first to describe this theory in detail, in his 1968 book, *Chariots of the Gods?*

Supposedly, ancient writings and carvings reveal alien encounters.

The book suggested that ancient people often mistook aliens for gods. Supposedly, ancient writings and carvings reveal alien encounters. In the Old Testament of the Bible, for example, Ezekial describes a vision of the heavens opening up and

a fiery chariot descending, carrying otherworldly beings. To Von Däniken, Ezekial actually witnessed aliens landing in a spacecraft. Von Däniken also interpreted this Mayan carving as an astronaut controlling a rocket. Others have used this same type of reasoning to propose that the Dogon story of the Nommo's ark describes an alien spaceship.

However, others disagree. In the case of the Mayan carving, archaeologists who have studied the culture say that the image is a king on his journey to the afterlife sitting on the tree that connects life and death. The stories about Ezekial and the Nommo more clearly describe flying crafts. But that does not imply that any real landing took place. They could simply have been works of fiction. People love to create fantasy worlds, myths, and legends. These often do not depict reality. But ancient alien theorists argue that extraterrestrials did more than visit Earth.

Supposedly, they also helped humans accomplish great feats of architecture, engineering, art, or science. For example, how did ancient people build incredible structures like Stonehenge in England or the Egyptian pyramids without heavy machinery? It may seem like aliens must have intervened.

## ✗

## THE POWER OF HUMAN EFFORT

The real answer is that building these structures took time, effort, and ingenuity. In 2016, a team of students from University College in London demonstrated a method people may have used to move massive stone blocks to Stonehenge. They placed a one-tonne stone block onto a wooden sledge, attached ropes, then rolled the sledge over a track made of logs. It took just ten people to move the load.

The pyramids are also a marvel of engineering. How did the Egyptians know how to build one?

The ancient Egyptians also used rollers, sleds, and their muscles to move the huge blocks that make up the pyramids. They left behind drawings showing themselves moving heavy loads in this manner. But the pyramids are also a marvel of engineering. How did the Egyptians know how to build one? The answer is that they developed techniques over the course of thousands of years. Early generations erected a tower of square blocks, called a mastaba. Finally, Egyptians attempted the first smooth-sided pyramids. At first, they did not succeed. At Meidum, you can see the remains of an early, collapsed pyramid. It doesn't look at all like something that technologically advanced aliens would build. Kenneth Feder, an archaeologist at Central Connecticut State University, says, "If these guys could traverse interstellar space they ought to do a much better job of piling up rocks." Still, as a scientist, he will always follow the evidence. "If tomorrow someone were to find a crashed flying saucer under the Sphinx, that would be really cool. I have no problem with that," he says. Until then, the evidence shows that ancient humans used their own creativity and intelligence to construct wonderful things.

# ANCIENT RITUALS

But what about the Nazca lines? It's intriguing to imagine that ancient people might have left behind a message to alien visitors. However, you don't have to fly over in an airplane (or space ship) to see the designs. Some of them are visible from the tops of hills surrounding the flat plain. Archaeological evidence also shows that the Nazca probably didn't make the lines for viewing. Instead, they walked along them during religious rituals and used some shapes as gathering sites. The remnants of offerings, including smashed pottery and seashells, have been found nearby. In addition, many of the lines seem to lead towards a site called Cahuachi, which contains temples and pyramids. It was likely a religious center and pilgrimage site.

*The remnants of offerings, including smashed pottery and seashells, have been found nearby.*

Several prominent scientists have also linked the Nazca lines to water. Barely any rain falls in the region, so the Nazca relied on several rivers. But for a few months every year, these rivers dry up. The Nazca built a series of aqueducts to provide enough water to survive. The lines may have pointed toward sources of water. They may also have been part of rituals intended to ask the gods for water.

Different designs and sets of lines may have served different purposes. And these purposes likely changed over time. However, there is one theory that links everything together. The designs may have all functioned as memory aids.

*The designs may have all functioned as memory aids.*

The Nazca were an oral culture. That means they had no written language. All of the information they had about water, animals, plants, farming, history, the motion of stars and planets, and more was carried in people's memories and passed from generation to generation. The easiest way to remember such detailed information is through song, or dance. Connecting pieces of information to landmarks or objects is another helpful method, says researcher Lynne Kelly, who studies oral cultures.

Modern people who participate in memory contests often imagine walking through a familiar house. Each room contains objects corresponding to something that person wants to remember, such as digits in a very long number. The technique works incredibly well. Kelly argues that techniques similar to this one were quite common among oral cultures around the globe. The Nazca and other cultures definitely walked on the lines. Perhaps walking these paths helped the Nazca remember important information.

## ✗ THE POWER OF HUMAN IMAGINATION AND INTELLIGENCE

The most convincing evidence of ancient aliens, aside from a crashed flying saucer, would be proof that aliens gave people knowledge or technology that they could not have come up with themselves. The story about the Dogon and Sirius B seems to be the perfect example of such knowledge. But when you look closely into the story, simpler explanations start to emerge.

*They easily could have read about astronomy themselves or learned about it from Europeans who visited the tribe.*

The rings around Saturn and moons of Jupiter aren't visible to the naked eye, but astronomers learned of them soon after Galileo pointed his first telescope at the night sky in 1610. And the existence of Sirius B was discovered in 1862, over sixty years before Griaule's visit with the Dogon tribe. Also, the tribe was not isolated. Dogon people served in the French army in Europe during World War I. They easily could have read about astronomy themselves or learned about it from Europeans who visited with the tribe. If the Dogon had known about the rings around Neptune, Uranus, and Jupiter, that would have been astounding. These weren't discovered until the 1970s and 1980s. But they didn't.

In addition, Griaule may have gotten the Dogon mythology all wrong. In the 1980s, another anthropologist, Walter E. A. van Beek, stayed with the Dogon. He found no evidence of any creation story, let alone one featuring fish-like spirits or flying arks. No one he spoke with knew that Sirius had an invisible twin star. But Van Beek noticed that his informants sometimes made up fanciful answers to his questions. For example, when he asked two men about Dogon names for colors, they started inventing names on the spot. Van Beek believes that Griaule may have unwittingly led Dogon elders to invent new, fictional myths. He may have accidentally fed them facts about astronomy along the way.

*Griaule may have unwittingly led Dogon elders to invent new, fictional myths.*

We may never know the truth behind the fantastic stories Griaule recorded, but one thing is clear. It's not true that only aliens could have revealed the existence of Sirius B to the Dogon. It's also not true that ancient Egyptians or Britons needed advanced technology to build incredible structures. And there are many intriguing reasons—besides signaling aliens—why the Nazca may have made giant designs on the desert.

The idea that any ancient civilization required extraterrestrial help diminishes their stunning achievements. "Human ingenuity can do things that are absolutely astonishing," says Luis Jamie Castillo Butters, an archaeologist at the Pontifical Catholic University of Peru who studies the Nazca lines. Ancient people came up with science, math, art, metallurgy, architecture, astronomy, memory techniques, and more. They did this with their own imagination and intelligence. That's truly out of this world.

*"Human ingenuity can do things that are absolutely astonishing."*

# WHEN THE DEAD RETURN

*A balding man with a scar on his cheek walks into a marketplace. He approaches a woman and says he's her brother. The woman is shocked. How is this possible? Her brother is dead.*

The man and woman, Clairvius and Angela Narcisse, reunited in 1980 in the small town of l'Estère, Haiti. Eighteen years earlier, Clairvius had gone to the hospital with a fever and had begun coughing up blood. Then he sank into a coma. A few days later, with Angela at his side, he took his last breath. Two doctors pronounced him dead. The next day, his family buried him.

But this man is very much alive. He tells Angela his childhood nickname, a name that only family knew. He also says that he remembers his burial. He could not speak or move, but he was aware. "Even as they cast dirt on my coffin, I was not there," Narcisse described later to researchers investigating his case. "My flesh was there, but I floated... I could hear everything that happened." Narcisse says that the scar on

*"Even as they cast dirt on my coffin, I was not there."*

his cheek comes from a nail inside the coffin. He also claims that after he was buried, a group of men came and took him from his grave. They beat him and brought him to a sugar plantation. He says he worked as a slave there for two years until the plantation owner died, and he escaped.

He says he didn't really die on that fateful day eighteen years ago. He became a zonbi.

# ✗
# ZONBI SLAVES

*A zonbi is a dead person returned to life, but it is not dangerous to other people. Rather, it is a slave with no will of its own.*

The word "zonbi" is spelled differently on purpose, to distinguish it from a "zombie." You've probably read books, watched movies, or played video games with zombie characters. Zombies are horrific monsters. They are mindless, walking corpses, hungry for brains or blood. The zonbis of Haiti inspired today's zombie stories. A zonbi is a dead person returned to life, but it is not dangerous to other people. Rather, it is a slave with no will of its own. In the Vodou religion of Haiti, zonbis are one small part of a much larger set of beliefs.

According to Vodou beliefs, a sorceror called a bokor has the power to turn people into zonbis. The process involves trapping a dead person's soul. In Vodou, each person has two souls. One is the life force in the body, and the other is that person's unique identity and willpower. This second soul is the one that a bokor captures to make a zonbi.

In most cases, the bokor never revives the dead body. Instead, he makes a zonbi of the spirit. This involves sealing the soul inside a bottle along with a variety of ingredients meant to bestow magical powers. A zonbi of the spirit supposedly brings good luck, beauty, fortune, and other benefits to its owner.

Anthropologist Elizabeth McAlister of Wesleyan University purchased one of these bottles early in her career, without knowing exactly what it was. She watched the bokor make it. "He burned an American dollar bill and put the ashes in the bottle... he poured the perfume in the bottle... and he took out from under his bed a human skull. And he proceeded to grate small shavings from the human skull and put those into the bottle." She later learned that the skull had been specially prepared in a ritual meant to extract its soul. The dollar bill tells the spirit to bring her wealth and the perfume is meant to keep her attractive.

*To make a zonbi of the body, a bokor supposedly poisons a victim with a magical powder.*

To make a zonbi of the body, a bokor supposedly poisons a victim with a magical powder. The victim sickens and seems to die. Right after the burial, the bokor digs up the body and revives the person as a zonbi. He also keeps the person's soul trapped in a bottle. Supposedly, he can use this captive soul to control the zonbi slave.

In 1973, French missionary Jean Kerboull was working in Haiti when he met Médélia, a person who claimed to be a zonbi. She recalled what happened to her: "I was thirteen years old... a strong ailment completely paralyzed me. In the morning, in everyone's opinion, I was dead... but I maintained enough

58

"In everyone's opinion, I was dead... but I maintained enough lucidity to realize what was happening to me..."

lucidity to realize what was happening to me... I heard the earth falling on my casket. And then, after a brief moment, I distinctly heard a voice crying out: 'Soul... earth!' And quickly, I found myself outside, standing between two young people, still conscious, but without will." According to lore, zonbis stare into space, speak very little or repetitively, and move in an awkward or clumsy fashion. They toil as slaves, but may escape if their souls are released or if they are allowed to taste salt.

Zonbi stories recall Haiti's disturbing history as a slave nation. The country was once the French colony Saint-Domingue, a leading producer of sugar and coffee. To grow these crops, plantation owners captured hundreds of thousands of people from Africa and forced them to work in horrific conditions. The slaves rebelled, and in 1804, won their independence. Yet in zonbi stories, slavery continues.

The belief in zonbis is so pervasive that the Haitian criminal code addresses it. If a poisoning leads to a state of near-death, and the victim is then buried, this is considered a murder. People sometimes take special steps to protect their dead, such as having the body cremated or guarding a new tomb at night. Still, cases similar to Narcisse's or Médélia's are occasionally reported in Haiti, even today.

## WHEN THE DEAD RETURN HOME

Wilfred D. died when he was just 18 years old, after suffering from an unknown illness. His family laid the body to rest in a tomb on a cousin's land. A year and a half later, the young man returned. His family says he recognized his father and remembered comments from the funeral. But he wasn't the same. They had to tie his legs to a log to keep him from wandering. He rarely spoke and needed help to bathe or change clothes. He occasionally experienced fits in which he cried out and thrashed his arms and legs. Everyone agreed he was a zonbi. In fact, his uncle was arrested and convicted of ordering the zonbification.

A woman identified only as MM also died at the age of 18 after taking part in prayers for a neighbor who everyone believed had been zonbified. Thirteen years later, she showed up in her home town. She said she'd been kept in a village 100 miles away and had given birth to a child there. After the bokor died, she walked home. She was not a typical zonbi since she spoke normally, laughed easily, and independently cared for herself. However, she was less intelligent than before her death. Her brother attempted to heal her with prayers.

What is going on in these stories and others like them? Have the dead really come back to life?

**✗**

## POISONED AND PARALYZED

It's a scientific fact that dead people do not return to life. But what if they were never dead to begin with? Author Zora Neale Hurston visited Haiti in the 1930s and met several people said to be zonbis. She wondered if bokors induced a death-like state using drugs. Beginning in the 1960s, the psychiatrist Lamarque

Douyon began tracking zonbi cases. He found Narcisse's story especially interesting. The death certificate in his name seemed to prove that he had died. DNA tests didn't exist yet, so Douyon interviewed Narcisse and his family. It seemed to Douyon that Narcisse knew too much about his former life to be an imposter. If he was the real Narcisse, then his death must have been faked. But how? Perhaps a bokor really had poisoned him, making him seem dead for a short period, then later revived him.

Drugs that bring a person very close to death without killing him or her are very useful. This is how some anesthetics keep a person unaware through surgery. A similar drug could potentially knock out astronauts for a long space journey. The possibility of discovering a new, powerful drug led a young scientist named Wade Davis to Haiti in 1982. While there, he purchased samples of zonbi powder from bokors in different parts of the country.

The ingredients certainly seemed creepy enough: bits of human bones, lizards, tarantulas, toads, sea worms, and dried puffer fish. Davis realized that most of these ingredients would have no meaningful effect on a person. But one stood out. Puffer fish contain a potent poison in their skin and some of their organs. That poison is tetradotoxin. "A lethal dose of pure tetradotoxin... would balance on the head of a pin," says Davis.

*Drugs that bring a person very close to death without killing him or her are very useful. This is how some anesthetics keep a person unaware through surgery.*

In Japan, some restaurants serve a species of puffer fish called fugu. Chefs must carefully remove the poisonous parts of the fish. Occasionally, people suffer from tetradotoxin poisoning after eating fugu that was not properly prepared. Symptoms include tingling around the mouth, difficulty breathing, weakness, nausea, and vomiting. A strong enough dose will paralyze the body, including the heart and lungs. This kills the person within a few hours. At just the right dose, Davis argues, tetrodotoxin may temporarily paralyze a person without killing him or her. The person may also suffer from brain damage, which could explain the mental impairments some zonbis have.

However, the powders that Davis brought back from Haiti did not contain enough tetradotoxin to harm a human being, let alone cause a death-like state. Experts in the effects of the poison argue that there is no scientific evidence that tetrodotoxin is behind the zonbi phenomenon. Zonbi powders definitely exist, but they likely have no serious effects. The truth behind each zonbi story is likely to be simpler, but just as surprising.

# ✗
# MISTAKEN IDENTITY

In Haiti, people often don't keep careful records of births, deaths, and other important life events. The hospital where Clairvius Narcisse supposedly died charged patients money for care. It's possible that someone who couldn't afford these fees used his name to check in, so the real Narcisse never died at all. But what about his family? They also claimed he had died. So perhaps there was no stranger who died under the wrong name. The family may have faked the documents because they no longer wanted him in their family. He had fathered several children and never supported them. He had also argued with his brother over land. Even after Narcisse returned eighteen years later, the family didn't really want him back.

In 1997, researchers analysed the cases of Wilfred D and MM. They did DNA testing, and found out that neither Wilfred D or MM were actually related to the families that had claimed them. They could not be the same people who had died. So what made the families accept them as their own? Both families had watched a teenager die. The loss must have been devastating. When each family later encountered a person who resembled the deceased young person, they welcomed them home. The idea that dead people may return as zonbis is part of Haitian folklore and culture. This fact combined with the families' grief at the untimely deaths likely made them open to the idea that their loved ones had returned.

To the relatives, the horrific process of zonbification also seemed to explain the impairments both young people had. However, the researchers actually diagnosed Wilfred D and MM with different mental illnesses. With MM's permission, the researchers brought her back to the place where she said she'd been held as a zonbi. People there recognized her as a local woman known to have a mental disorder. She seemed to have simply wandered away from home. In these cases, the belief in zonbification offers a way to understand and sometimes care for people with mental illnesses. Haiti's population struggles with poverty and many illnesses go untreated. If someone with a mental illness is recognized as a zonbi, then in some cases, he or she may end up adopted into a family willing to care for him or her.

Haitian culture and the families' grief at the untimely deaths likely made them open to the idea that their loved ones had returned as zonbis.

It seems that the real mystery of the zonbi is not about the dead somehow returning to life, but about understanding Haitian culture and the Vodou religion. The real power of zonbis of the spirit, zonbi powders, and even zonbis of the body lies in the strength of human belief.

# AMAZING POWERS OF THE MIND

*A tall young man with striking features and thick black hair hunches over a piece of paper, pen in hand, eyes closed. He's about to demonstrate remarkable and mysterious powers of the mind.*

The year is 1973, and the young man is Uri Geller. He's appearing on a live television talk show that was very popular in Britain at the time. Before his appearance, a production assistant for the show retreated into a closed room, made a picture of some unknown object, and hid it in an envelope. Geller says he can use the powers of his mind to see it. He doesn't know how he does it. Maybe he reads the thoughts of the production assistant, a power called telepathy. Or maybe his mind probes inside the envelope to see the drawing hidden within, an ability called clairvoyance.

*Maybe his mind probes inside the envelope to see the drawing hidden within, an ability called clairvoyance.*

"OK, I'm getting something," Geller says, resting one hand on the sealed envelope sitting on the table in front of him. He begins to draw, a large triangle over a long, thin horizontal shape. "It could be a boat or a ship," he says. The talk show host opens the envelope. Out comes a drawing of a sailboat, almost identical to the one Geller just made. The audience cheers.

*Out comes a drawing of a sailboat, almost identical to the one Geller made.*

Geller has more amazing abilities. Later on the same show, he picks up a fork and begins to rub it between his fingers. "I'm holding it very, very gently," he says, and the camera zooms in on his fingers. After a few minutes, he says, "It's cracking. Look, it's becoming like plastic. It's breaking." The end of the fork falls to the floor with a clatter. In similar performances around the world, he bends or breaks spoons, keys, rings, and other metal objects. He stops or starts watches and influences the behavior of other machines.

He claims that he does this with the power of his mind, an ability called telekinesis.

In multiple radio and television appearances, Uri Geller tells his audience to try these same feats at home. Surprisingly, many people report that metal objects in their homes bend mysteriously, or that broken watches or other machines suddenly start working again. One woman in San Francisco had a watch that once belonged to her grandfather. It hadn't worked for many years and she always kept it in her dresser drawer. But after watching Geller on TV, she found the watch on her bed. In a letter, she reports, "It was running!!! It had been transported some way from the drawer to the bed while I was in the living room!"

Could psychic powers be real? In a book about his life, Uri Geller wrote, "I feel that these powers come from far outside me, that I am like a tube that channels them... I know that something unusual is going on here, and I'd like other people, as many as possible, to know about it, to explore it together."

*"I feel that these powers come from far outside me, that I am like a tube that channels them"*

✗

## SCIENTISTS INVESTIGATE

Geller and his audiences aren't the only ones exploring the possibilities of psychic phenomena. Over the decades, some scientists have tried to determine if telepathy, clairvoyance, telekinesis, and other powers are real. And if they are real, then how do they work? What unknown forces or energies might be involved? In 1970, during the Cold War between the USA and the Soviet Union, American spies obtained a video of secret Soviet research.

In the film, a woman named Nina Kulagina seemingly stopped a beating frog's heart using only the power of her mind. She also seemed to be able to lift and move small objects with mental powers. The video alarmed the US Defense Department. Could psychics stop peoples' hearts from afar? What else could they do? Might they alter the thoughts of US leaders or disable US military equipment? The US Central Intelligence Agency (CIA) decided to take action. They planned an investigation into psychic phenomena.

*Could psychics stop peoples' hearts from afar? What else could they do?*

Two excellent physicists, Hal Puthoff and Russell Targ, agreed to perform the research. They worked with Uri Geller and several other psychics on a series of experiments during 1972 and 1973 at the Stanford Research Institute (SRI). During one series of experiments, Geller tried to reproduce hidden drawings. For most of these trials, Geller sat locked inside a room surrounded by double walls of steel. This was meant to prevent him from seeing or hearing anything going on outside the room. Once he was locked in, researchers outside selected an object and made a drawing. When the researchers drew the solar system, Geller also produced a picture of planets. Remarkably, when the researchers drew a bunch of grapes, Geller produced a picture with the exact same number of grapes on it.

*"We have observed certain phenomena with the subjects for which we have no scientific explanation."*

In a presentation to fellow scientists following these studies, Targ said, "We have observed certain phenomena with the subjects for which we have no scientific explanation." A year later, the study appeared in *Nature*, one of the world's most prestigious science journals. Geller told his adoring fans that his abilities had been scientifically proven to be real.

# MAGIC TRICKS

In fact, the scientific evidence was shaky. *Nature* had published a detailed commentary alongside the study. This cautioned that the experiments were not well designed or carefully conducted. It was impossible to rule out trickery as an explanation. *Nature* hoped that publishing would help quiet down rumors that SRI had made a breakthrough.

Only Geller knows what really happened at SRI, or during his many public appearances. And he continues to maintain that he has real powers. However, magicians say otherwise. Many of them have duplicated Geller's feats. Spoon bending, for example, is a simple trick that anyone can easily learn. You can find videos on YouTube showing you how to do it without any supernatural powers. During that 1973 talk show appearance, Geller may have done it using a large metal belt buckle that he wore. While the audience was distracted, he could have easily snuck a fork into his lap and bent or broke it with one hand using the buckle for leverage. While he strokes the fork, his fingers never leave one spot at the utensil's neck. Most likely, the fork is already broken there, but the audience believes it is whole.

*Spoon bending is a simple trick that anyone can easily learn.*

Geller likely used tricks for his hidden drawing demonstrations, too. On the 1973 talk show, a production assistant made the drawing earlier in the day. Geller and his helpers had plenty of time to sneakily figure out what it was. In the SRI experiments, though, the scientists made the pictures only after Geller was locked inside the room. However, the room contained an audio link to allow the scientists to hear Geller. Supposedly, he could not hear them. But Geller's assistant and longtime friend, Shipi Shtrang, was present during the experiments. James Randi, a famous magician, suspects that Shtrang found some way to give Geller clues.

*Shtrang may have slipped a copy of the grapes drawing through the hole.*

Perhaps the pair hacked into the audio line. Or maybe Geller made up excuses to temporarily leave the shielded room, and looked for subtle gestures or mouthed words from Shtrang. Randi also discovered that the double-walled steel room had a small hole to allow electrical cables in. Shtrang may have slipped a copy of the grapes drawing through the hole.

During several of the drawing experiments, no one had any way to know what the picture was. For example, in one experiment, an artist not connected to the research made 100 pictures and other people sealed these inside of double envelopes. Then, the research team selected one of these at random. Geller refused to try to draw the selected picture. Targ admitted that the experiments were not well controlled. He said, "Geller manipulates the experiments to a degree of chaos where he feels comfortable and where we feel uncomfortable."

The James Randi Educational Foundation offers a million dollar prize to anyone who can prove any sort of psychic ability... Many have tried, but none have succeeded.

But what if an experiment is well controlled? Have scientists found any convincing evidence of psychic abilities? The James Randi Educational Foundation offers a million dollar prize to anyone who can prove any sort of psychic ability following their strict testing procedures. Many have tried, but none have succeeded.

## ✗
## THE LURE OF BELIEF

Sometimes, Uri Geller wound up in a situation where he couldn't resort to tricks. In 1973, he appeared on *The Tonight Show* with Johnny Carson. This was one of the most popular shows in America at the time. Beforehand, James Randi told Carson to provide his own props for the show and not to let Geller or his team near them in advance. During the show, Geller did nothing. He didn't bend any spoons or copy any hidden drawings. He said, "I'm having a hard time with you... I don't feel strong." This failure didn't matter at all to Geller's fans. He always approached tests of his abilities with a shy, nervous demeanor, saying that his powers didn't always work. It was easy to like him and really want him to succeed. This desire to believe helps explain the cases where Geller's audiences report using mental powers to bend spoons or repair broken watches at home. Clearly, no magic trick could affect a spoon or watch located in a home many miles away. So what was really happening?

Many of the unusual events were coincidences. In a show with hundreds of thousands or even millions of viewers, something strange will happen in some of the homes during the show.

These people wanted to believe Uri Geller, so they assumed he somehow caused the strange thing to happen. (Or perhaps they went so far as to make up a strange event.) Of course, for the vast majority of viewers, nothing special happened. But these cases didn't get reported. So everyone only heard about events that supported the idea that psychic powers are real.

However, some people really did manage to start broken watches or bend spoons. How did they do it? Holding or shaking a stopped watch will often make it tick again—temporarily. This seems magical to people who don't know how watches work. Also, most people never try to bend utensils or keys. So they wrongly assume that this must be very difficult to do. But it's not. Susana Martinez-Conde, a neuroscientist at SUNY Downstate Medical Center in New York, remembers watching Geller on TV as a child. She went into the kitchen, grabbed a spoon, and rubbed her fingers along the neck. To her surprise, it started to bend! But it wasn't telekinesis. "I noticed I was bending it by exerting pressure on it," she says. She wanted the spoon to bend, so she had forced it without really meaning to. This likely happened to other viewers as well. Some assumed that the power of the mind—not the fingertips—bent the spoon.

You may have experienced unusual events in your life. Perhaps you sometimes have dreams that later come true. Or maybe mechanical objects seem to fail around you. Or perhaps you always know which friend is going to text you next. Do these sorts of experiences mean that the human mind has mysterious powers?

Of course, for the vast majority of viewers, nothing special happened. But these cases didn't get reported.

Some assumed that the power of the mind—not the fingertips—bent the spoon.

73

People often build up beliefs based on events that seem related but are not. "Our brain is a meaning-seeking machine," says Martinez-Conde. Normally, linking together causes and effects helps people form useful beliefs about the world. For example, dark clouds lead to rain and thorns lead to painful pricks. But this same process also leads to false beliefs and superstitions, like the idea that wearing your lucky hat or shirt or socks can help your favorite sports team win a game.

*Normally, linking together causes and effects helps people form useful beliefs about the world.*

People also tend to notice and remember only evidence that supports existing beliefs. At the same time, they ignore or explain away evidence that conflicts with beliefs. This is called confirmation bias. If you believe that your dreams predict the future, you will remember dreams that match future events, but will ignore or forget the majority of dreams that don't.

✗

## OPEN YOUR PALM

Most psychics believe in their own abilities. "They are fooling themselves as much as everybody else," says Christopher French, a psychologist at Goldsmiths University of London.  Uri Geller may use tricks in his performances but still truly believe that he has real powers that only work occasionally. Other psychics may not consciously use any tricks at all. They usually meet one-on-one with clients to help them figure out how to handle problems in their lives or to plan for the future. Psychics may study the lines on the palm, an arrangement of cards, or the date of a person's birth.

*If he saw that a person's heart line was broken, then that person had indeed experienced a broken heart.*

When Ray Hyman was a teenager, he learned to read palms. He just wanted a way to make some extra money. But his readings worked so well that he became a believer. If he saw that that the line on a person's palm called the heart line was broken, then the person always said that they had been unlucky in love. A few years later, a friend challenged him to tell his clients the exact opposite of what he saw in their palms. If the heart line was broken, he had to say that the person was in a happy relationship. Strangely, the readings still worked!

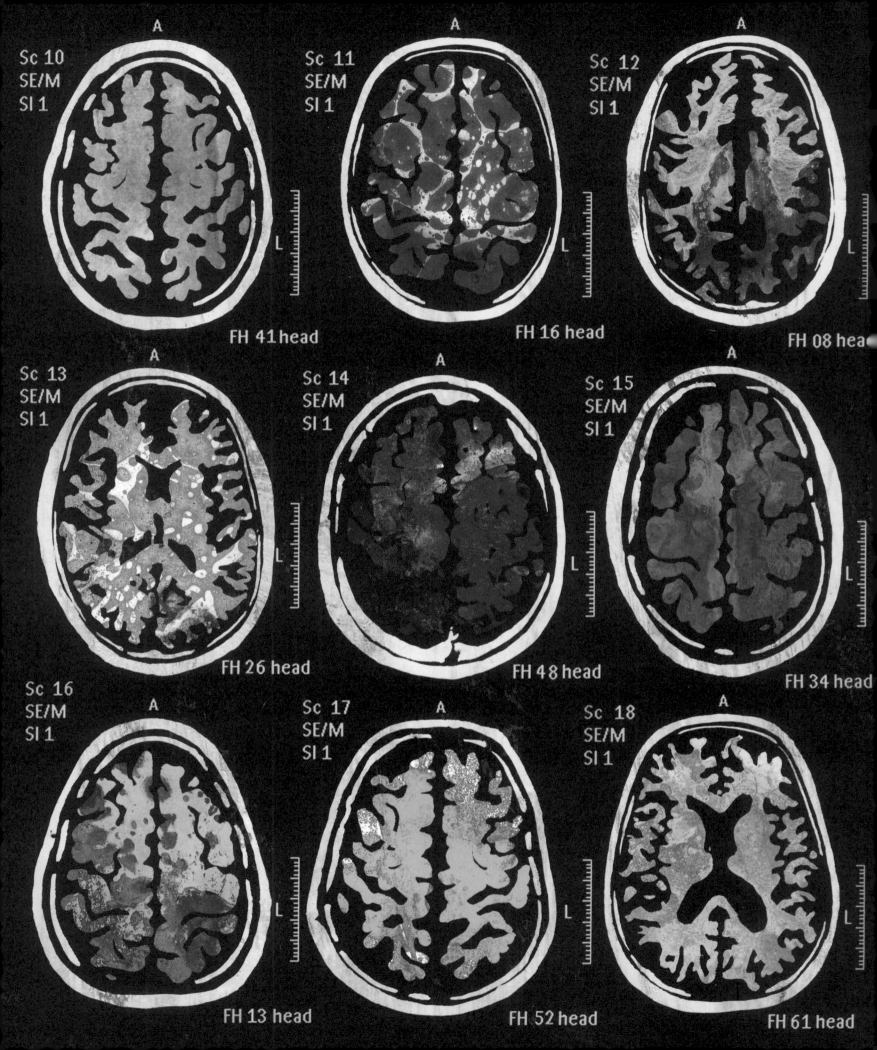

Hyman is now a psychologist at the University of Oregon who debunks claims of psychic ability. He says he learned an important lesson from this early experiment. "If you set people up right, you can tell them anything. If they've got a creative and intelligent mind, then no matter how crazy it seems to be, they can find a way of reinterpreting it so it really fits them like a glove."

The psychic and client work together to come up with a meaningful story. The psychic often begins with vague statements that apply to anyone. For example, "You are shy at times, but also have a great time going out with friends." A person who is not very shy ignores the first half of this sentence, but may smile and nod during the second half. So the psychic can continue on using this information. If the psychic gets something completely wrong, he or she can change the story until the client responds positively. If the psychic says, "I see a long trip on a boat," and the person has never been on a boat, no harm done. The psychic can say that the boat is a metaphor for travel. Or maybe a boat trip is in the future. Or maybe a loved one has spent time on a boat. The ultimate effect is that the reading feels magical. But the real magic is in the creativity and adaptability of the human mind.

*Scientists who study the brain are beginning to understand and decipher some of its patterns.*

# ✗
# THE FUTURE OF MIND READING

Real psychic abilities do not seem to exist. But this doesn't make the human brain any less amazing and mysterious. It is an organ that sparks with electricity as billions of cells called neurons communicate with each other. Patterns of flashing neurons control the body and form thoughts, emotions, dreams, and more. Scientists who study the brain are beginning to understand and decipher some of these patterns. People who are paralyzed or who have lost limbs have learned to control a robotic arm or leg with their thoughts. This seems like telekinesis! But in fact, a computer system translates messages from the brain into instructions that move the arm or leg. Other researchers have collected brain activity as people watched movies. They managed to recreate blurry images of the movies from patterns in the brain activity. These brain-computer systems can't read entire thoughts like reading a book. But in the future, it's certainly possible that people could gain powers very similar to telepathy. If this ever happens, it will be science and technology that make it possible.

# THE SECRETS OF AN ANCIENT TOMB

*A desolate desert ravine cuts through steep cliffs across the Nile river from what was once the grand city of Thebes. Thousands of years ago, ancient Egyptians buried their kings here, in tombs dug deep into the rocky ground.*

A rchaeologists call this place the Valley of Kings. On the morning of November 4, 1922, a team of workers toils here, slowly excavating a pile of sand and rock with picks and shovels. Their leader, archaeologist Howard Carter, has been methodically digging his way across the valley for a total of six years, looking for any sign of a tomb. This year, his frustrated sponsor, Lord Carnarvon, was ready to call it quits. But Carter convinced him to fund one last season.

This is his last chance to find something. And today, he finally does. One of the workers discovers the corner of a stair. As the team clears rubble, it becomes clear that the buried staircase leads down to the entrance to a tomb. The next day, Carter notes in his diary, "It was a thrilling moment for an excavator... to suddenly find himself, after so many years of toilsome work, on the verge of what looked like a magnificent discovery—an untouched tomb."

Lord Carnarvon, waiting for his own turn to look, asks if he can see anything. Carter famously responds, "'Yes, wonderful things.'"

Lord Carnarvon travels to Egypt to witness its opening. First, Carter makes a small hole in the doorway and puts a candle through. He later wrote, "As my eyes grew accustomed to the light, details of the room within emerged slowly from the mist, strange animals, statues and gold—everywhere the glint of gold." Lord Carnarvon, waiting for his own turn to look, asks if he can see anything. Carter famously responds, "Yes, wonderful things."

This was an archaeologist's dream come true. But could Carter and Carnarvon have made a terrible mistake in opening the sealed tomb? Over the next months and years, people connected with the opening of the tomb meet untimely and unusual deaths. Could the archeologists have accidentally triggered an ancient curse?

## THE MUMMY'S CURSE

*They made him a beautiful mask of gold and gems, then placed the mummy into a solid gold coffin and sealed that inside a whole series of elaborate containers.*

The newly discovered tomb belonged to Tutankhamen, a pharaoh of ancient Egypt. He died in the 1320s BC when he was just 18 or 19 years old. As was the tradition in Egypt at the time, embalmers removed the young king's organs and mummified his body. They made him a beautiful mask of gold and gems, then placed the mummy into a solid gold coffin, and sealed that inside a whole series of elaborate containers in the underground tomb. The ancient Egyptians believed that people live on after death in another realm and can bring items from this world along with them. So they filled the rooms next to the young king's burial chamber with couches, chairs, clothing, chariots, vases, and other treasures. Over the next three thousand years, grave robbers broke into many ancient Egyptian tombs and looted their treasures. But most of the rooms in this tomb remained sealed and untouched, completely hidden underground, until that fateful day in 1922.

News of the astonishing discovery captivated the world, and the boy king in the pure gold coffin was nicknamed "King Tut." But in early 1923, just a few weeks after the tomb was officially opened to the world, tragedy struck. Lord Carnarvon became seriously ill. The novelist Marie Corelli speculated that breaking into a tomb that was never meant to be opened had somehow caused his illness. In fact, a mosquito bite on his cheek had become infected. But when Lord Carnarvon died in April in Cairo, Egypt, the idea of an ancient curse took hold. Some sources reported that at the moment of his death, the lights went out in the city. Supposedly, back home in Britain, his dog howled and died instantly. Sir Arthur Conan Doyle, creator of the Sherlock Holmes mysteries and a believer in spiritualism, blamed the death on an "evil elemental," another term for a spirit. Had something in the tomb killed Lord Carnarvon? Was it King Tut's spirit seeking vengeance?

*Just a few weeks after the tomb was officially opened to the world, tragedy struck.*

Bite of an Insect Develop into Pneumonia

DISCOVERED TOMB OF TUTANKAHMEN

TOMB DIGGING TO GO ON DESPITE CURSE OF EGYPT

A PRIES OF DE

The curse seemingly took many more victims. George Jay Gould, a wealthy American railroad executive, reportedly visited the tomb in 1923 and then died soon after of a fever. Later that same year, Lord Carnarvon's half-brother, Aubrey Herbert, died of complications after surgery. His friends reported that he had objected to opening the tomb, and recalled him saying, "Something dreadful will surely happen in our family." Also in 1923, the Egyptian prince Ali Kamel Fahmy Bey was murdered by his wife on a trip to London. He had reportedly visited the tomb. Hugh Evelyn-White, one of the archaeologists who worked with Carter, committed suicide in 1924. And these are just a few examples. One newspaper reported that people were so afraid of ancient curses that they started sending Egyptian artifacts back to museums, fearful that keeping them would lead to an untimely demise.

*His friends reported that he had objected to opening the tomb, and recalled him saying, "something dreadful will surely happen in our family."*

Ancient Egyptians definitely did not want people messing with their tombs. They occasionally left threatening messages. According to archaeologist Zahi Hawass, one inscription reads: "O all people who enter this tomb, who will make evil against this tomb and destroy it, may the crocodile be against them in water and snakes against them on land. May the hippopotamus be against them in water, the scorpion against them on land." Hawass says that he found this inscription on a tomb located near the Pyramid of Giza. This tomb houses thousands of workers and several supervisors who were responsible for building the pyramid during the 2500s BC.

## Museum Sends Back Cursed Artifacts

# THE LURE OF A GOOD STORY

However, King Tut's tomb contains no inscribed curses, anywhere. So why were people so quick to believe that one existed? One of the reasons is that they already believed that Egyptian mummies brought bad luck.

In the 1800s, Egyptomania swept through Britain. Egyptian artifacts—especially mummies—were in demand. Some people even attended mummy unwrappings for entertainment. By the end of the century, though, scientists began to focus on carefully preserving mummies and other artifacts. In 1889, the British Museum received the gift of a decorated mummy board, illustrated on the right. It had served as the inner lid of a mummy's coffin. According to the legend, five young men had purchased it on a trip to Egypt in the 1860s, and two of those men died on the way home from the trip.

Another accidentally shot himself while hunting in Cairo and lost an arm. Another lost his fortune gambling. By the time the artifact arrived at the museum, it already had a reputation for wreaking havoc. Then, in 1904, an article in the *Daily Express* told the story of the cursed board, stating, "It is certain that the Egyptians had powers which we in the 20th century may laugh at, yet can never understand."

So by the time King Tut's tomb was opened, Britain was already used to the idea of vengeful mummies. In addition, the press needed a good story to tell. Lord Carnarvon had made an exclusive deal with *The Times*, a London-based newspaper. Only reporters from this one paper had access to the inside of the tomb and the artifacts found there. But every paper wanted to carry news of the exciting discovery. So when Lord Carnarvon died, they jumped on the idea of a curse, and put out story after story. Some of the things they reported seem to be rumors rather than facts. The British Museum, for example, has no record of a flood of returned artifacts. The news about Lord Carnarvon's dog dying when he did has never been verified. And if the lights did go out in any part of Cairo, this was not unusual. Power outages were a regular occurrence at the time. But the curse made for a good story, so it seems that reporters bent the facts to fit.

*By the time the artifact arrived at the museum, it already had a reputation for wreaking havoc.*

*Some of the things they reported seem to be rumours rather than facts. The British Museum, for example, has no record of a flood of returned artifacts.*

Also, there's one glaring problem with the curse theory. Howard Carter lived a long life. He died of cancer at age 65, seventeen years after discovering the tomb. He had spent nearly fifty years of his life searching for and exploring the tombs of ancient pharaohs. If Egyptian curses had any real power, he should have been a prime target. So why didn't he meet an untimely end?

# THE TRUTH BEHIND THE CURSE

Perhaps vengeful spirits aren't to blame for the deaths. However, could there be a scientific reason for them? Some have proposed that mold, bacteria, or other toxins in the tomb may have played a part. In fact, mummies may carry harmful mold and dangerous bacteria may make their home on tomb walls. It seems like a sound, scientific theory that these substances may have sickened some of the people on Carter's team. But dangerous mold and bacteria grow in many other places as well. During the time period the tomb was discovered, people weren't as careful about sanitation and cleanliness. Cities were a haven for germs. As many experts in disease have pointed out, the archaeologists excavating King Tut's tomb were likely safer from disease inside the tomb than outside! Plus, many of the deaths attributed to the curse had nothing to do with germs. Some were murders or suicides.

*Some have proposed that mold, bacteria or other toxins in the tomb may have played a part.*

What if the opening of King Tut's tomb and the deaths weren't connected at all? When investigating a mystery, you should always assume that events are unrelated until proven otherwise. This is called the null hypothesis. A pharaoh's tomb was excavated, and a number of people died, some in unusual ways. But these facts may have nothing to do with each other. In other words, it could be a coincidence. But aren't there too many deaths related to King Tut's tomb to be explained away as coincidences?

*A number of people died, some in unusual ways. But these facts may have nothing to do with each other. In other words, it could be a coincidence.*

In 2002, Mark Nelson, an epidemiologist (a scientist who studies disease) carried out a scientific study to look into the curse. He found forty-four non-Egyptian people who were all in Egypt when Carter opened King Tut's tomb. He divided them into two groups. The exposed group of twenty-five entered the tomb, witnessed the opening of the nested coffins, or helped examine the mummy. The rest did not join in any of these activities. Then, he looked at how long people in each group survived. People in the exposed group were no more likely to die early than those who had had no contact with the tomb. So the numbers suggest there was never a curse at all. There were simply different, unrelated reasons for the deaths. For example, Lord Carnarvon's health had been failing for a long time. It was a coincidence that he passed away so soon after the tomb was opened.

# ✖
# BURIED MYSTERIES

**Archaeologists must respect the wishes of any descendants of the dead.**

Most archaeologists aren't scared of curses, but they still approach the study of ancient tombs and burial grounds with caution and respect. That's because ethical issues surround the study of dead bodies, even ancient ones. Archaeologists must respect the wishes of any descendants of the dead. In addition, they realize that entering a tomb or removing items often leads to damage and a loss of information about the site. Today, they mainly focus on preserving items where they are found. For example, an open space in the Great Pyramid may contain a hidden room. But opening the room might cause irreversible damage. So the space remains an unexplored mystery.

In China, another buried mystery awaits exploration. The first emperor, Qin Shihuang, united multiple warring states into one nation, China, in 221 BCE. Archaeologists know the location of his tomb, but it has never been excavated. Historian Sima Qian, writing a hundred years after Qin Shihuang's death, described the tomb as filled with treasures, including a miniature map of the empire with rivers and oceans of mercury on the floor and stars and planets made of pearls and gems on the ceiling.

**Though archaeologists know the location of his tomb, it has never been excavated.**

To protect the tomb, this account says, builders rigged crossbows to shoot at anyone who dared try to enter. Sima Qian also wrote that the emperor killed many of the slaves and craftspeople who labored on the tomb, in order to protect its secrets. At least some of this description seems to be true, as archaeologists have found high levels of mercury around the tomb and pits filled with the bodies of laborers.

And in 1974, farmers digging a well a short distance away from this tomb happened upon unusual figures molded from terracotta (a type of fired clay). Archaeologists discovered three pits filled with an estimated 8,000 archers, infantry, cavalry, charioteers, and generals, along with their weapons and horses. They are life-sized, with facial features that seem unique. Most likely, they were placed there to guard the first emperor and his treasures in the afterlife.

*In 1974, farmers digging a well a short distance away from this tomb happened upon unusual, life-sized figures molded from terracotta.*

It seems that the emperor did not want anyone stealing his treasures or disturbing his monument. And so far, he has had his wish. Xiuzhen Li, an archaeologist who studies the terracotta army, says, "Many people wish to see the treasures inside, to see the mysteries inside, but we cannot." Opening the tomb would mean disrespect to a figure who is very important in Chinese history and might damage the artifacts inside. So Li and her colleagues are hoping that future technology will allow them to see inside without disturbing the contents. What will they find? She has no idea. No one ever expected to find an army of almost 8,000 life-sized warriors. Sima Qian did not even mention them in his history. The mysteries awaiting in the main tomb could be truly fantastic—perhaps even more incredible than the piles of gold in King Tut's tomb.

*Opening the tomb would mean disrespect to a figure who is very important in Chinese history and might damage the artifacts inside.*

89

# LOST AT SEA

*Clouds gather in a moonless night sky as jet engines roar to life on a runway below. "Cleared for takeoff," radios the air traffic control tower.*

The airplane soars from the island country of Malaysia out over the South China Sea on its way to Beijing. Air traffic control instructs the plane to contact the next tower in Vietnam. Then, at 1:19 AM on March 8, 2014, the pilot signs off with his flight's name and number, saying, "Good night Malaysian three seven zero." That is the last message the plane transmits. It never contacts the next tower and it doesn't land in Beijing at its scheduled time of 6:30 AM. No one hears from the 12 crew members or the 227 passengers on board, ever again. The mystery deepens when experts review radar and satellite data. These show that the plane, called MH370, did not simply crash. It veered off course and then flew for another seven hours after losing radio contact. Where did it end up?

Experts' best guess is that the plane eventually crashed and sank into the Indian Ocean, about 1,500 miles west of the coastal city of Perth, Australia. But why? Was it a deliberate act of terror? Or was there an accident, like an electrical failure or a fire? Anguished families of the lost crew and passengers have waited years for answers. Yet they have none. Despite a series of massive searches, no one has found MH370. How could an entire airplane full of people vanish?

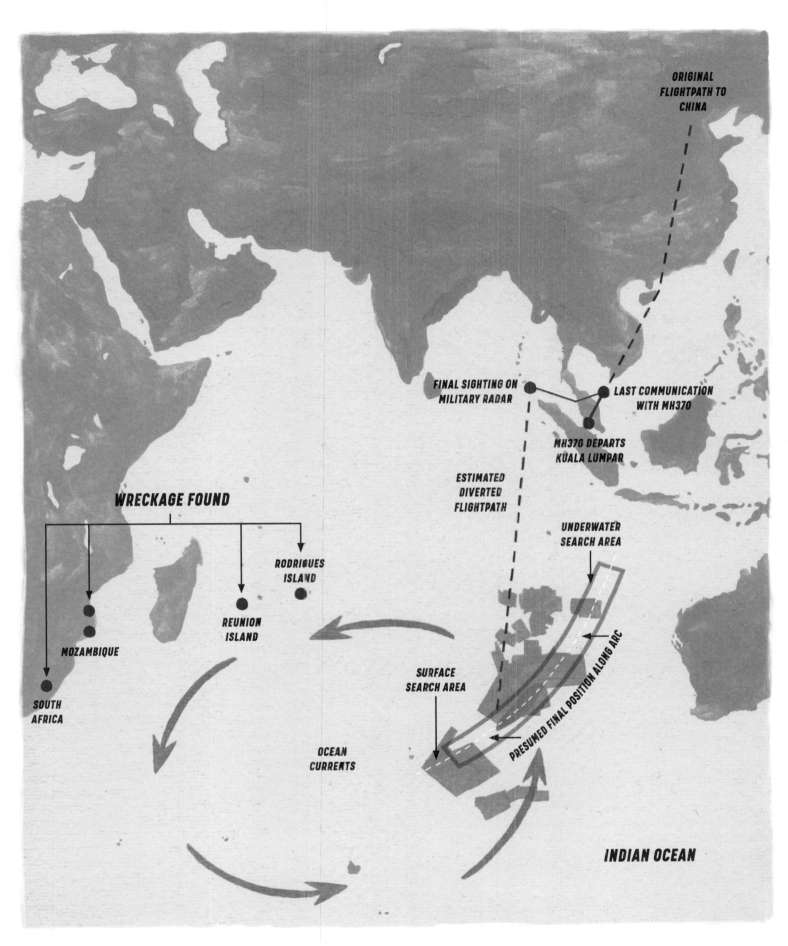

ORIGINAL
FLIGHTPATH TO
CHINA

FINAL SIGHTING ON
MILITARY RADAR

LAST COMMUNICATION
WITH MH370

MH370 DEPARTS
KUALA LUMPAR

ESTIMATED
DIVERTED
FLIGHTPATH

WRECKAGE FOUND

UNDERWATER
SEARCH AREA

RODRIGUES
ISLAND

REUNION
ISLAND

MOZAMBIQUE

SURFACE
SEARCH AREA

PRESUMED FINAL POSITION ALONG ARC

SOUTH
AFRICA

OCEAN
CURRENTS

INDIAN OCEAN

Despite a series of massive searches, no one has found MH370.

## THE BERMUDA TRIANGLE

Airplanes and ships have disappeared before. On the exact opposite side of the globe from Perth, Australia sits the island of Bermuda. This small island marks the tip of a region known as the Bermuda Triangle. In most accounts, Miami, Florida and San Juan, Puerto Rico are the other points of a triangle that covers approximately 500,000 square miles. According to legend, this area is especially dangerous for ships and aircraft, and no one knows why. Some who have passed through safely report experiencing strange things, such as unusual weather or malfunctioning compasses and other equipment.

*Some who have passed through safely report experiencing strange things, such as unusual weather or malfunctioning compasses and other equipment.*

The story of the mysterious triangle began on December 5, 1945. At 2:10 that afternoon, five TBM Avenger torpedo bombers took off from Fort Lauderdale, Florida on a routine training mission labeled Flight 19. They planned to fly east out over the Atlantic, drop practice bombs, turn north and fly over part of the Bahamas islands, and finally head southwest back to base. It was a clear sunny day and all of the planes were in fine working order. The mission should have lasted two hours. But Flight 19 never returned.

"*I don't know where we are. We must have got lost after that last turn.*"

Almost all of the fourteen pilots and crewmembers aboard the five planes were students. Their instructor and the leader of the mission, veteran pilot Lt. Charles C. Taylor, sent a series of alarming radio messages beginning at around 3:40 pm. He said, "I don't know where we are. We must have got lost after that last turn." Later he radioed, "Both my compasses are out." By the time ground stations figured out Flight 19's position, it was too late. They couldn't reach Taylor with instructions. That evening, two search planes loaded with

rescue gear took off to try to find the missing bombers. One of the search planes failed to return. A massive search followed, but never found any wreckage.

What happened to Flight 19 and the search plane? Could something menacing lurk in the waters off the coast of Florida? And could that same something explain other mysterious disappearances, perhaps even that of MH370?

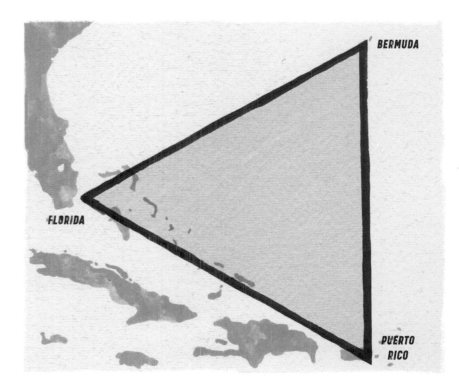

BERMUDA

FLORIDA

PUERTO RICO

# A LEGEND IS BORN

In 1964, a fiction story titled "The Deadly Bermuda Triangle," ran in *Argosy* magazine. The story named the triangle for the first time, described many incidents of lost planes and ships, and said, "This relatively limited area is the scene of disappearances that total far beyond the laws of chance." Ten years later, Charles Berlitz published *The Bermuda Triangle*, a hugely popular book that brought the mystery to life in the minds of the general public.

*"This relatively limited area is the scene of disappearances that total far beyond the laws of chance."*

Supposedly, mysterious disappearances in or near the Bermuda Triangle can be traced back far into the past. In the 19th and early 20th century, a number of ships vanished on trips through or near the Bermuda Triangle. The HMS *Atalanta* disappeared on a training voyage. The ship arrived in Bermuda in January 1880, but never made it back to England. Despite a massive search, no trace of the ship was ever found. Joshua Slocum, the first man to sail alone around the world, was 65 when he left on a trip that took him through the Bermuda Triangle in 1909. He also never returned.

*He made it out of the mist, but later realized that a flight that should have taken well over an hour had only lasted forty-seven minutes.*

Many airplanes have vanished in the region, too. The airliner Star Tiger was lost near Bermuda on January 30, 1948, and a DC-3 passenger plane went down near Miami, Florida later that same year after experiencing electrical problems. A final report investigating what may have happened to the Star Tiger concluded that "some external cause may overwhelm both man and machine... what happened in this case will never be known..." In December 1970, pilot Bruce Gernon says that he was flying over the Bahamas when he went through a swirling tunnel in a cloud and found himself in a gray mist that seemed to prevent the plane's electronic and magnetic instruments from functioning. He made it out of the mist, but later realized that a flight that should have taken well over an hour had only lasted forty-seven minutes.

Supposedly, a single mysterious force or phenomenon links all of these events and many more. Gernon says it is electronic fog, and believes it forms within thunderstorms. Supposedly this fog can disable navigation equipment and even trigger time warps or travel through alternate dimensions. Others believe that crystal pyramids that once powered the lost city of Atlantis lurk beneath the sea, sending out occasional bursts of energy that take down planes and ships.

An astrophysicist checked Gernon's story and determined that a strong tailwind could explain the shortened flight. Wormholes that might lead to another time or dimension are theoretically possible, but have never been found. It would most likely be impossible for a human to travel through one. And no one has found any evidence that Atlantis ever existed, let alone crystal pyramids.

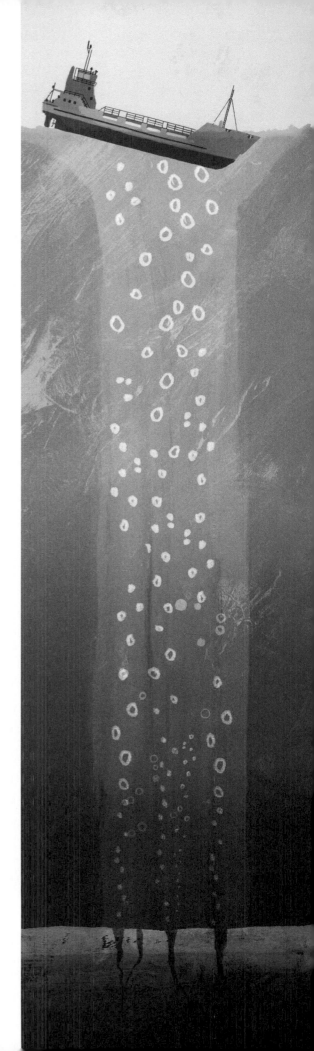

*Giant bubbles of gas sometimes rise up from the sea floor, and scientists have shown that if a ship happens to be above such a bubble when it reaches the surface, the ship might get sucked down and sink.*

If these theories seem too wild, plenty of practical ones exist. For example, giant bubbles of gas sometimes rise up from the sea floor, and scientists have shown that if a ship happens to be above such a bubble when it reaches the surface, the ship might get sucked down and sink. Rogue waves, massive walls of water more than twice the size of surrounding waves, are also real and may occur in the Bermuda Triangle region. Scientists are still working to understand this phenomenon. Or perhaps an unusual weather event called a microburst is to blame. This produces a brief blast of strong winds. Some argue that there is not one Bermuda Triangle, but several, dotting the world's oceans with danger zones. Perhaps MH370 went down in one of these regions.

✗

## IS IT REALLY A MYSTERY?

*Before looking for a solution to a mystery, you need to make sure that a mystery exists.*

All of these explanations, even the practical ones, miss one very important thing. Before looking for a solution to a mystery, you need to make sure that a mystery exists. Remember the null hypothesis? The disappearances blamed on the Bermuda Triangle may not be connected to each other. The National Ocean Service says there is no evidence of an unusually large number of incidents in this area. It seems that ships and planes are just as likely to vanish in any large, well-traveled part of the ocean. Many accidents have happened in the Bermuda Triangle simply because many planes and ships have traveled there. However, the vast majority of the people who fly or sail through the Bermuda Triangle arrive safely at their destinations. Commercial airlines and shipping companies take no special precautions in the region. If you've flown to or from Miami, Florida, you likely passed through the Bermuda Triangle.

*Taylor had recently transferred from flying missions out over the Florida Keys, and seems to have confused one set of islands for the other.*

In most cases, a practical explanation exists for the disappearances. Tragic human error seems to explain the disappearance of Flight 19. The planes had planned to fly over the Bahamas, a chain of islands to the east of Florida. But Taylor had recently transferred from flying missions out over the Florida Keys, and seems to have confused one set of islands for the other. In one of his radio transmissions, he said, "I'm sure I'm in the Keys… I don't know how to get to Fort Lauderdale." The Florida Keys extend southwest from the tip of Florida. So Taylor planned to head north, thinking that would take him back to land. However, he was not where he thought he was. Intercepted messages between some of the student pilots reveal that they realized the problem. "If we would just fly west we would get home," one said. By the time ground stations finally located Flight 19 north of the Bahamas, they could not reach the planes with instructions to turn west. The pleasant afternoon had transformed into a dark, stormy night. What about the search plane that disappeared that evening? A nearby ship witnessed an explosion. The plane likely went down when fumes from its huge gas tanks caught fire.

Bad decisions, foul weather, and equipment failures explain almost all of the disappearances associated with the Bermuda Triangle. No evidence exists to connect them to each other. In some cases, investigators have not been able to figure out exactly what went wrong. But this doesn't make theories about electronic fog or crystal pyramids any more likely. The truth is perhaps more straightforward. They are all tragic accidents.

*Bad decisions, foul weather, and equipment failures explain almost all of the disappearances associated with the Bermuda Triangle.*

# THE MISSING JET

It may seem unfathomable that a huge jet like MH370 could disappear. But when you look at all the facts, it makes sense that searchers haven't found it. "That big airplane is nothing but a tiny dot on the ocean," says John Goglia, an aviation safety expert. Plus, search and rescue teams started out looking in the wrong place—the location of the last radio communication, which was over the South China Sea. It took time for experts to analyze the radar and satellite data and discover that the plane had made several turns and continued to fly for hours. Once they started looking in the Indian Ocean, a month had passed. Any wreckage would have already sunk or dispersed on the waves. And the ocean floor in this area is full of mountains and valleys. It is not easy to search there. Over the years, a few pieces that likely came from the plane have washed up on beaches on Madagascar and nearby islands. This confirms that the main wreckage is most likely somewhere beneath the Indian Ocean.

*Over the years, a few pieces that likely came from the plane have washed up on beaches on Madagascar and nearby islands.*

But how did the plane end up so far away from where it was supposed to be? A few scenarios seem most likely. Goglia believes that a person sabotaged the flight on purpose. "That person could have been one of the flight crew or somebody else on the airplane," he says. The plane's transponder—a device that sends information about the plane's position—stopped working minutes after the pilot's final radio message. Perhaps someone turned it off. Also, the plane's first few turns followed what seems like a deliberate path between two countries' airspace, as if someone was trying to avoid detection. However, no evidence has been found to show that the pilot or co-pilot was suicidal, or that anyone on board had a motive to hijack the airplane.

What about an accident? If there was a fire, the plane wouldn't have been able to fly on for hours afterwards. But another type of accident makes some sense. High in the sky, airplanes must maintain cabin air pressure so passengers can breathe. If that pressure drops, the people on board must put on oxygen masks and a pilot must bring the plane down to a safe altitude. If this doesn't happen, everyone will eventually pass out and die. Before they pass out, they will experience hypoxia, a condition that occurs when the brain lacks oxygen. Hypoxia causes a number of bizarre symptoms, including blissful feelings as well as impaired vision, judgement, coordination, and memory. Basically, you feel fine, but can't think straight or make rational decisions.

An electrical failure on board MH370 could have explained the shut down transponder. Another system that communicated with a satellite also shut down, but started up again later, likely automatically. It was this system that allowed experts to track the plane to the Indian Ocean. Whatever caused the electrical failure may have also caused a drop in pressure. The pilots may have attempted to turn around and fly back to Malaysia. But once they began suffering from hypoxia, they would no longer be able to make good decisions. They may have made a few turns, then passed out. In this scenario, the plane became a ghost ship, eventually running out of fuel after flying on autopilot for hours.

While the plane remains missing, no amount of theorizing and guessing will reveal the real truth of what happened. The evidence investigators need sank to the bottom of a vast, deep, unforgiving ocean. The oceans have swallowed up the secrets of many disasters over the years. Someday, hopefully, the wreckage of these ships and planes will come to light, revealing evidence that leads to the solution to an unsolved mystery.

# THE MYSTERY OF DEAD MOUNTAIN

*A single tent sits on a snowswept mountain slope, almost invisible in the dark and silent winter night. Inside, nine young hikers rest, protected from the frigid weather outside.*

I t's February 1, 1959, deep in the Ural Mountains. The hikers are university students in the Soviet Union, now the country of Russia. Their trip into the Ural Mountains is supposed to take sixteen days or longer, in the dead of winter, in one of the most remote and forbidding landscapes in the world. However, all of them are experienced hikers. They feel excited and ready for the challenge. Zinaida ("Zina") Kolmogorova, one of the hikers, wrote the day before they departed: "I wonder what awaits us in this hike? Will anything new happen?"

Suddenly, something disturbs the peace. The hikers slice through the wall of the tent from the inside. They leap out into the darkness, in such a hurry to escape that most of them do not put on jackets or shoes.

*"I wonder what awaits us in this hike? Will anything new happen?"*

On February 26th, a search-and-rescue mission finds the hikers' tent, abandoned and damaged. The next day the searchers discover footprints leading away from the tent, down toward the edge of nearby woods. That same day they find the first bodies. But it will take months of searching through deep snow to find the remains of all nine people. Investigators are mystified. Two of the hikers started a fire and broken branches on a nearby tree indicate that they attempted to climb it. Their bodies are found clothed only in underwear and socks. Five of the hikers died of exposure to the cold, but suffered from injuries as well, including burns. Four died of broken ribs, fractured skulls, and other serious injuries that indicate a sudden, crushing impact. The lead investigator, Lev Ivanov, under pressure from the government to close the case, determined that "an unknown compelling force" led to the deaths.

The next day, they discover footprints leading away from the tent.

That is not a very satisfying explanation. In the decades since the deaths, many people have continued to try and solve the mystery of what happened. It has become known as the Dyatlov Pass Incident, after Igor Dyatlov, the leader of the group. Some have traveled to the mountain where the hikers died. Author Keith McCloskey is one of them. He said the strangest thing about the place was an eerie quiet. Other than occasional strong gusts of wind, "it was just still, completely still. You didn't hear any animals or birds or anything. Just absolute silence." The mountain's name is Kholat Syakhl, which means "Dead Mountain" in the language of the native people. What could have terrified the young hikers enough to force them out of the safety of their tent and into the bitter cold of this remote place?

*Other than occasional strong gusts of wind, "it was just still, completely still."*

✗

## WIND, FIRE, OR AVALANCHE

Some sort of natural disaster would be the simplest and most likely explanation. At first, the search team blamed high winds, which were common in the area. But if the wind was strong enough to blow away people, the tent should have blown away, too. Some people have wondered if the stove inside the tent started a fire. This would have explained the burns found on two of the hikers. However, the hikers never actually assembled the stove that night, and experts think the burns most likely happened when the two hikers passed out over the fire they had built under the tree.

*What about an avalanche? They're common in the Ural Mountains.*

What about an avalanche? They're common in the Ural Mountains, and could certainly have caused broken ribs and fractured skulls. However, the slope where the tent stood was not very steep, meaning that an avalanche on that particular slope was extremely unlikely. Plus, the tent was found still standing, not buried in snow. Investigators haven't found a clear natural reason for the deaths. So some have come up with wilder theories.

# GLOWING ORBS

Other hikers in the Ural Mountains during February 1959 noticed strange, glowing orbs in the sky. Residents of the nearby town of Ivdel also reported unusual lights. These facts get UFO enthusiasts very excited. Could alien visitors have something to do with the tragedy?

In fact, the incident happened during the Cold War when the Soviet Union was developing and testing new weapons technology. During February and March 1959, the country launched missiles that would have been visible in the Ural Mountains. The Soviet military was also testing parachute mines. These bombs explode in the air close to the ground. The blast causes internal injuries such as broken ribs, like the hikers had. Perhaps a military accident killed the hikers, and the government covered it up? Lev Ivanov, lead investigator for the case, said after his retirement, "I can't tell for sure whether those orbs were weapons or not, but I'm certain that they were directly related to the death of the hikers." But other experts aren't so sure. The orb sightings and missile launches occurred during the middle of the month and the hikers died on the night of February 1st. So what else could be the cause?

# THE MONSTER OF THE MOUNTAIN

Maybe an animal disturbed the hikers that night, and they tried to get away. The Ural Mountains are home to large, dangerous predators including wolves, wolverines, and brown bears. However, this group of experienced hikers would have known that if an animal threatens, the worst thing you can do is leave the safety of your tent. But what if it was an animal that the hikers weren't familiar with?

*On one hiker's camera, the last image shows a dark figure.*

Something that they found so scary, they didn't think straight? When the bodies were recovered, their personal belongings were too, including their cameras. And on one hiker's camera, the last image shows a dark figure that resembles a large beast. The group also put together a newspaper the same night that they died. In it, they wrote, "According to recent reports, Yeti lives in the Northern Urals."

What is a yeti? The legend began in the Himalayas, a mountain range at the border of Nepal and Tibet, far away from the Ural Mountains. In the 1900s, a number of European explorers ventured to the area, determined to reach the summit of the  world's highest peak, Mount Everest. Some of them brought back stories from the locals of a beast called a yeti. During a 1921 expedition, Lieutenant Colonel Charles Kenneth Howard-Bury of the British Army came across a strange set of footprints. The local guides told him these were made by a metoh-kangmi, a term for a mountain animal. In English newspapers, though, the phrase was mistakenly translated to "abominable snowman." Now, explorers had a new motive. They still attempted to conquer the world's highest peak. But they also searched for one of the world's most elusive creatures.

*Howard-Bury of the British Army came across a strange set of footprints.*

In 1952, a zoologist named Bernard Heuvelmans came up with a theory that the yeti evolved from *Gigantopithecus*, a giant ape that once lived in southern China. It stood 10 feet tall, resembled an orangutan, and likely walked on all fours. 100,000 years ago, it went extinct. Some people have seized on Heuvelmans' idea and argued that descendants of this giant ape spread out all across Asia—including Russia, where the hikers were found—and also into North America. In North America, the theory goes, the creature became known as Sasquatch, or Bigfoot.

'Snowmen' Enormity Is Terrifying

Hideous Monster
Baffles Science

World Stunned by
18-inch Footprint

Female Bigfoot
Captured on Video!

Man Frightened To Death
By 'Abominable Snowman'

The earliest recorded Bigfoot encounter happened in 1811, when explorer David Thompson came across a set of massive footprints in the snow in Alberta province, Canada. Over the years, many others have collected casts of gigantic prints, hair, or droppings. People have also reported sightings. In 1924, a group of gold prospectors in Washington state shot at a hairy, ape-like creature in the woods. Fred Beck later described it as "seven feet tall with blackish-brown hair." Late that night, as the men slept in their cabin, the creatures came back for revenge. They threw rocks and "pushed against the walls of the cabin as if trying to push the cabin over," Beck said of the terrifying ordeal. The sightings continue to this day. For example, Dustin Teudhope says he encountered a bigfoot while out hunting in Florida in 2009. "On two feet it resembles a werewolf," he says.

*They threw rocks and "pushed against the walls of the cabin as if trying to pull the cabin over."*

These are only a few out of hundreds of reported Bigfoot and yeti encounters. These monsters certainly seem scary enough to have terrified a group of hikers. In 2014, a Discovery Channel documentary argued that a yeti was responsible for the Dyatlov

Pass deaths. Why? The injuries on the hikers were so severe that it seemed only a creature with superhuman strength could have caused them. Plus, the two hikers who tried to climb a tree could have been attempting to escape from something. But what does the evidence say?

## ✗
## THE DNA SPEAKS

When you look at the evidence, a beast attack of any kind seems unlikely in the Dyatlov Pass incident. Some of the hikers' footprints were found, but no animal prints. Plus, the injuries don't match the slashes or bites of a typical animal attack. The tent was ripped from the inside, not the outside, so a creature didn't try to get in. Also, the newspaper the group put together was clearly a joke, with many humorous or sarcastic articles. And most people believe that the dark figure in the photo was likely one of the hikers wearing a winter coat.

Also, the idea that creatures like the yeti or bigfoot exist at all is doubtful. Most serious scientists shy away from the subject. Bryan Sykes, a geneticist at Oxford University in England, thought this was too bad. "Science doesn't reject anything," he says. "It just examines the evidence for and against." After all, it wasn't completely out of the question that a small population of ape-like creatures might live, undetected, in a remote part of the world. So Sykes and other scientists examined hair, bone, tooth, and other samples that supposedly came from yeti or bigfoot. They used the same DNA analysis methods that police and detectives use. But everything came from ordinary animals, often bears. The bigfoot prints that Thompson found could have come from bears too. And human pranksters have admitted to planting many other large footprints. The cabin attack may also have been people playing a mean trick. Most likely, any huge beast lurking in the snowy Himalayas is a bear, not an abominable snowman. The myth probably grew out of real experiences with bears. In fact, the word "yeti" comes from the word "yeh-teh," meaning "snow bear" in an old Tibetan dialect.

*Most likely, any huge beast lurking in the snowy Himalayas is a bear, not an abominable snowman.*

# ✘
# AN UNSOLVED MYSTERY

If it wasn't a yeti or a natural disaster, what did cause the hikers to run out of their tent into the freezing cold, all those years ago? Some wonder if a bad fight or argument broke out, and some of the group either ran away or stormed off. Then the others may have tried and failed to rescue them. Another intriguing theory blames infrasound. Some militaries around the world have experimented with infrasound weapons, since the sounds may make some people feel anxious, sad, afraid, or even terrified. But the sounds can also occur naturally. When high winds blow around an obstacle of a certain size or shape, the wind swirls into a series of tiny tornadoes that roar with real sounds as well as infrasound. And the top of the mountain near where the hikers pitched their tent was the perfect shape for this effect, according to experts. Perhaps these sounds drove the hikers from their tent in a panic. and they couldn't find their way back in the dark. They may have stumbled and fallen, fatally injuring themselves. Could this be the real reason they died?

The truth is that we may never know. However, there is always a chance that new evidence might be discovered, both in the Dyatlov Pass case and in the search for Bigfoot and other mythic monsters. As believers like to say, the absence of evidence is not evidence of absence. In other words, just because we haven't found Bigfoot yet doesn't mean we never will. But we need proof. Every mystery has an explanation. Getting to the bottom of it is what science is all about.

*There is always a chance that new evidence might be discovered.*

# MONSTERS OF THE DEEP

*The submersible dives down, deeper and deeper. The color of the surrounding water fades from blue green to rich blue and finally to gray-black. Suddenly, out of the blackness, a jellyfish covered with dancing lights appears.*

I t's a lovely sight. But the people inside the bright yellow Triton submersible are not looking for small creatures, no matter how flashy. They have come to the Ogasawara islands of Japan on this summer day in 2012 to search for a massive beast.

*It grabs prey using eight long arms and two even longer feeding tentacles.*

Its eyes are each the same size as a human head. It grabs prey using eight long arms and two even longer feeding tentacles. With these tentacles stretched out, it can reach the height of a four-story building. On each of its arms and tentacles, hundreds of suction cups with sharp, serrated edges cut into whatever it grabs. It devours each meal with a sharp beak and toothed tongue.

Inside its body, three hearts beat, pushing blue blood through the creature's veins. And its skin changes color, shimmering through hues of metallic silver and bronze. Should any other creature try to attack it, the beast sprays out a cloud of jet-black ink. This cloaks its escape. On this dive, the group fails to find what they're looking for. But they will keep trying. What is this monster they seek? Could it possibly be real?

*And its skin changes color, shimmering through hues of metallic silver and bronze.*

# THE KRAKEN

Sea monsters have swum through myth and folklore as far back as the 13th century, when *The Saga of Arrow-Odd*, an Icelandic romance, mentioned a beast called Hafgufa that swallowed men and ships. In 1555, Olaus Magnus, an archibishop in Sweden, described and illustrated several sea monsters, writing that one of these beasts could drown many great ships. In 1755, bishop Erik Pontoppidan described the kraken, a beast so large it resembles a string of small islands. He wrote it was "round, flat, and full of arms, or branches." When a kraken rises to the surface, he writes, smart fishermen "take to their oars and get away as fast as they can."

One of these beasts could drown many great ships.

> *"Monstrous arms like trees seized the vessel and she keeled over."*

In 1874, the *London Times* published an account of a huge, squid-like beast attacking a ship called the *Pearl* in the Indian Ocean. According to this story, a passing vessel rescued the captain, James Floyd, and several crew members. Floyd reported that "Monstrous arms like trees seized the vessel and she keeled over; in another second the monster was aboard..." Next, the crew apparently fought the beast with axes, but in the end, it pulled the ship under water. Could all of these stories have some truth to them? Does a monstrous squid lurk beneath the ocean? The people in the Triton thought so, and they intended to find it.

# PREHISTORIC SURVIVORS?

Lakes also seem to hide their own secret monsters. Hundreds of millions of years ago, long before the first legends of the kraken, large reptiles known as plesiosaurs dwelled in the world's oceans as well as in some freshwater lakes. Fossil evidence shows these very real water monsters became extinct around 65 million years ago along with many dinosaurs. However, some wonder if a few populations managed to survive, undetected, in the oceans or in very deep lakes.

*People have reported seeing unusual creatures in bodies of water around the world and some have captured photographs or videos of their encounters.*

People have reported seeing unusual creatures in bodies of water around the world and some have captured photographs or videos of their encounters. Typically, these beasts resemble serpents. They often have a long neck or a serpentine body that rises from the water in a series of arches. In 1934, a photo showing what looked like a head and neck rising from Loch Ness in Scotland made a creature called Nessie famous. And in 1937, whalers pulled a strange-looking creature from a sperm whale's stomach. It had a camel-like head, a long body, and flippers. Some say it was a young sea serpent, nicknamed Cadborosaurus.

Today in North America, "Champ" of Lake Champlain in New York

and "Ogopogo" of Lake Okanagan in British Columbia have their own circles of believers and supporters. In 1977, Sandra Mansi's children were playing in the water of Lake Champlain when something broke through the surface near the middle of the lake. It looked like the head and neck of a large beast. "I could see that it was living," she later said. Her fiancé called the kids out of the water while she took a photo. It seems to show a curving neck, head, and the top of the body of the creature called "Champ."

*It looked like the head and neck of a large beast. "I could see that it was living," she later said.*

Over at Lake Okanagan, native people told stories of a supernatural being called N'ha-a-itk that lurked beneath the water. To get across the lake safely, the legend goes, travelers had to toss a chicken or other small animal overboard as a sacrifice to this supernatural being. In a retelling of one story, a chief named Timbasket refused to offer a sacrifice because he didn't believe the monster existed. As he crossed the lake, "Suddenly, the lake demon arose from his lair and whipped up the surface of the lake with his long tail. Timbasket, his family and his canoe were sucked under by a great swirl of angry water." These stories reportedly go back hundreds of years before the arrival of settlers from Europe. Today, though, the creature in the lake has a new name, "Ogopogo," and a reputation as a harmless, reclusive beast.

John Kirk, president of the British Columbia Scientific Cryptozoology Club, has seen what he believes to be Ogopogo with his own eyes on several occasions. (Cryptozoology is the name for the study of animals such as Bigfoot that are not proven to exist.) During one of his sightings, he says that five black humps appeared, along with a tail that seemed to lash up and down. The creature seemed to be almost as long as a school bus. "Because of my own personal experience, I know something lives in that lake," he says.

In 1991, a Japanese TV crew sponsored a search of the bottom of the lake using a submersible. The pilot saw nothing, but he did notice a long, straight groove in the lake floor. A long, thin creature could have made such a mark while resting on the lake bottom. Kirk believes the submersible pilot narrowly missed an underwater sighting of the mysterious creature.

## ✘
## DRIFTWOOD, OTTERS, AND MORE

Could descendants of plesiosaurs still survive in some lakes and oceans? Though the evidence Kirk and others have gathered may seem convincing, it's not enough. Stories, photographs, and even videos do not guarantee that a creature exists. Many things get mistaken for lake monsters, says Joe Nickell, an investigator who looks into these types of mysteries. Common culprits include bobbing logs, a diving bird called a cormorant, odd-looking waves, schools of fish, otters, and more. The long, straight impression on the floor of Lake Okanagan could have come from a giant creature, but it also could have been a log.

An oddly shaped piece of driftwood could explain Sandra Mansi's sighting. She stated that the creature never moved its head, though she watched it for several minutes. Eventually, it sank back under the water. It didn't dive or move around like a living creature probably would. Also, out on a lake, it's difficult to tell an object's distance, so it may appear larger than it really is. So perhaps Mansi was mistaken. The "creature" could have been neither alive nor gigantic.

The Nessie photo also shows something of indeterminate size, but there is an even bigger reason why it can't be considered to be real evidence: it turned out to be a hoax. One of the people who produced the famous photo later came forward and admitted it was fake—he and several others had attached a plastic head and neck to a toy submarine. With today's technology, it's even easier than ever before to create fake photos and videos that help feed the myth of Nessie and other monsters.

*From a distance, a group of otters swimming and playing together may look like one, connected, snake-like creature.*

Often, though, people do see unidentifiable living creatures in lakes. But these are more likely to be known animals than unknown ones. For example, the humps and tail John Kirk saw could have belonged to otters. When an otter dives, its body arches above the surface. From a distance, a group of otters swimming and playing together may look like one connected, snake-like creature. In fact, Nickell spoke with wildlife technician Jon Kopp who was out banding ducks when he witnessed something strange. At first it seemed like a serpent, but as it approached, he realized it was a group of otters diving and surfacing.

119

As with bigfoot and the yeti, scientists need a specimen, dead or alive, to determine whether lake and sea serpents are really a new, undescribed species of animal. Some claim the unusual serpent-like body found in 1937 counts. At the time, though, experts identified it as a whale fetus, and more recently scientists have said it could be a decomposed shark or a pipefish. There isn't enough evidence to suggest that it is something unknown to science.

# ✗
# THE REAL KRAKEN

*Dead bodies of large, many-armed sea creatures with toothy suction cups and giant eyes have been washing up on beaches for hundreds of years.*

When it comes to the kraken, though, the story has a very different ending. Sailors and fishermen are famous for telling tales. Many stories of the kraken veer far from reality. For example, the existence of the *Pearl* and its captain has never been verified. Nickell discovered that the *London Times* reprinted the story of a kraken attack on a ship from a British paper in India. Most likely, the story is fiction, inspired by author Jules Verne. His hugely popular science-fiction book *Twenty Thousand Leagues Under the Sea*, published five years before the London Times story, described an almost identical battle in which a ship's crew wielded axes against a huge, many-armed creature.

However, it's also true that dead bodies of large, many-armed sea creatures with toothy suction cups and giant eyes have been washing up on beaches for hundreds of years. The earliest known record comes from Iceland in 1639. The description of the creature states that it had seven tails densely covered with a type of button. These were likely tentacles with suction cups. In 1673, another one washed ashore in Ireland. Carl Linnaeus, the scientist who founded the modern method of classifying animals, described the kraken as a cephalopod mollusk in 1735. And in 1853, after the body of a huge, dead squid washed up on a beach in Denmark, naturalist Japetus Steenstrup recovered the beak, and used it to give the species a new name, *Architeuthis monachus*, the giant squid. A few years later, fishermen in Newfoundland managed to recover a tentacle and gave it to naturalist Reverand Moses Harvey. In an 1899 article, he wrote, "I was now the possessor of one of the rarest curiosities in the whole animal kingdom—the veritable tentacle of the hitherto mythical devilfish, about whose existence naturalists have been disputing for centuries." Clearly, the kraken was not as huge or bloodthirsty as the legends made it out to be. But it was real. It was the giant squid. Still, the creature remained shrouded in mystery. As of 2012, no one had ever seen one alive in its natural habitat. That was about to change.

# ✘
# AN ALIEN ENCOUNTER

The Triton descends once more. This time, marine biologist Tsunemi Kubodera of the National Museum of Nature and Science in Tokyo is on board. Dim red lights peer into the surrounding water. Most deep ocean animals can't see the deepest shades of red. But they can see the bait, a three-foot-long squid tied to a string that trails from the sub. It sports a flashing light lure.

*Then, out of the blackness, something appears. It reaches for the bait with long, suction-cupped arms.*

Two hours pass. Then, out of the blackness, something appears. It reaches for the bait with long, suction-cupped arms. "It's a giant squid! We've done it!" An excited Kubodera says in Japanese. He takes a chance and turns on the sub's bright white lights, but the creature does not swim away. It feeds for 23 minutes as Kubodera and his colleagues watch, in awe. They are the first humans to come eye to eye with a giant squid in the deep sea. When it finally leaves, Kubodera leans back, staring upwards. All he can say is, "Oh!"

There's no doubt about it. The giant squid is a real sea monster. And even more amazing, unknown creatures likely remain hidden in Earth's oceans. We have better maps of the surface of Mars and Venus than of the ocean floor. What could be down there? No one knows. Edith Widder, a marine biologist who took part in the expedition that filmed the giant squid, says that she welcomes any opportunity to explore the world's lakes and oceans. Exploring "opens up possibilities of seeing things we couldn't have imagined are there."

Every day, scientists explore the world, seeking the answers to unsolved mysteries. It took centuries of scientific research and experimentation to finally reveal the giant squid hiding behind the mystery of the kraken. What other mysteries remain to be discovered and solved? The only way to find out is to get out there and look.

# END NOTES

## An Encounter With Aliens

My main source for the story of Betty and Barney's encounter and for the history of UFO sightings: Donald R. Prothero and Timothy D. Callahan. *UFOs, Chemtrails, and Aliens: What Science Says.* Indiana University Press: 2017.

p. 11: "It's a recreation in your brain..." James McGaha. Personal Interview. July 25, 2018.

p. 13: Jim Macdonald tells the story of the light on Cannon Mountain in this podcast: Martin Willis. "278. Free Show: Jim MacDonald." Podcast UFO Live, November 29, 2017. https://podcastufo.com/podcast/278-free-show-jim-macdonald/

p. 13 I'd like to thank Experiencer Lisa Galarneau for sharing her personal encounters.

p. 15: "I woke up around 3AM..." and "I found myself waking up..." Susan A. Clancy. *Abducted: How People Come to Believe They Were Kidnapped by Aliens.* Harvard University Press, 2007. p. 34-35

p. 16: For more information on how memories change and how false memories can be created, see the work of Elizabeth Loftus, a psychologist at the University of California Irvine.

p. 18: Read more about Marjorie Fish's investigation of Betty Hill's star map here: Terence Dickinson, "The Zeta Reticuli (or Ridiculi) Incident." *Astronomy*, December 1974, reprinted with commentary by John Wenz, November 3, 2016. http://astronomy.com/bonus/zeta

p. 19: This article explains the scientific theories about the Hessdalen lights in detail: Caroline Williams. "Norse UFOs: What are the glowing orbs of Hessdalen?" *New Scientist*, May 7, 2014. https://www.newscientist.com/article/mg22229680-600-norse-ufos-what-are-the-glowing-orbs-of-hessdalen/

p. 21: "We are beginning..." James Oberg. Personal Interview. July 25, 2018.

p. 21: "There are billions and billions..." Eddie Irizarry. Personal Interview. August 21, 2018.

## The Haunted Mansion

p. 22: "I always felt like someone..." and p. 33: "If you come to our place..." Lawrence Ryan. Personal Interview. August 15, 2018. Ryan was also my main source for the history and ghost stories associated with the Monte Cristo Homestead.

p. 28: Read more about William H. Mumler's ghost photography here: Colin Dickey. "The Broken Technology of Ghost Hunting." *The Atlantic*, November 14, 2016. https://www.theatlantic.com/science/archive/2016/11/the-broken-technology-of-ghost-hunting/506627/

p. 30: "In all our years..." Noah Leigh. Personal Interview. September 4, 2018.

p. 30: The late neuroscientist Michael Persinger extensively investigated the relationship between electromagnetic fields and paranormal experiences.

p. 31: Here is the study describing researchers' attempt to build a haunted room: Christopher C. French, et al. "The "Haunt" project: An attempt to build a "haunted" room by manipulating complex electromagnetic fields and infrasound." *Cortex*, Vol. 45, Issue 5, May 2009. p. 619-29.

p. 33: "It doesn't matter what you and I believe..." Joe Nickell. Personal Interview, August 30, 2018.

## The Search for Lost Worlds

My main source on the history of the Atlantis myth: Kenneth L. Feder. *Frauds, Myths, and Mysteries: Science and Pseudoscience in Archaeology.* Mountain View, California: Mayfield Publishing Company, 1990.

p. 36: "Then listen, Socrates..." Plato. Timaeus. 360 BCE. Translated by Benjamin Jowett, The Internet Classics Archive, 1994-2009. http://classics.mit.edu/Plato/timaeus.html

p. 36 The illustration is based on a map made by Athanasius Kircher in 1675.

p. 37: "I am much disposed to believe..." William O'Connor. "Elusive Atlantis Never Loses its Allure." *The Daily Beast*, March 21, 2015. https://www.thedailybeast.com/elusive-atlantis-never-loses-its-allure

p. 38: "In the sunken portions..." Edgar Cayce. "Reading 440-5." Edgar Cayce's Atlantis Readings, 1933. https://www.bibliotecapleyades.net/esp_cayce_4.htm

p. 38: "And Poseidia will be among..." Edgar Cayce. "Reading 958-3." Edgar Cayce's Atlantis Readings, 1944. https://www.bibliotecapleyades.net/esp_cayce_4.htm

p. 41: "At first sight..." and "That was about the time..." Eugene Shinn. Personal interview, June 20, 2018.

## The Star of Deep Beginning

p. 46: Griaule retells stories from Dogon mythology in this book: Marcel Griaule and Germaine Dierterlen. *The Pale Fox*, Stephan C. Infantino, translator. Continuum Foundation, 1986.

p. 49: "signs to beings..." Erich von Däniken. *Chariots of the Gods? Unsolved Mysteries of the Past.* New York: Berkley Books, 1999. p. 18.

p. 50: The illustration depicts the sarcophagus lid of K'inich Janaab' Pakal, a Mayan king who lived during the 7th century.

p. 51: This research demonstrated how people can move heavy loads on sledges: Barney Harris. "Profile: Moving Stonehenge." Public Archaeology,

Vol. 15, 2016. Published online April 19, 2017. https://www.tandfonline.com/doi/abs/10.1080/14655187
.2016.1261250

p. 52: "If these guys could traverse..." and "If tomorrow someone..." Kenneth Feder. Personal Interview.
May 30, 2018.

p. 53: For information on the Nazca lines and their purpose, I spoke with Donald Proulx, an anthropologist
at the University of Massachusetts, and Luis Jaime Castillo Butters, an archaeologist at the Pontifical
Catholic University of Peru.

p. 53: The archaeologist and mathematician Maria Reiche studied the Nazca lines for almost her entire life
and believed they were an astronomical calendar.

p. 53–54: Lynne Kelly presents her ideas about memory techniques in her book: Lynne Kelly.
*The bMemory Code: The Secrets of Stonehenge, Easter Island and Other Ancient Monuments.* Pegasus Books, 2017.

p. 55: Walter E.A. Van Beek questions Griaule's interpretation of Dogon mythology in this paper: Van Beek,
Walter E.A., et al. "Dogon Restudied: A Field Evaluation of the Work of Marcel Griaule." Vol. 32, No. 2, April
1991. https://www.jstor.org/stable/2743641

p. 55: "Human ingenuity..." Luis Jaime Castillo Butters. Personal Interview. June 13, 2018.

## When the Dead Return

For information on Vodou and zonbis, I spoke with Elizabeth McAlister, a religious studies scholar at
Wesleyan University. This book was another important source: Phyllis Galembo. *Vodou: Visions and Voices
of Haiti.* Ten Speed Press, 2005.

p. 56: "Even as they cast dirt..." Wade Davis. *The Serpent and the Rainbow.* New York: Simon and Schuster.
1985. p. 81.

p. 58: "He burned an American dollar bill..." and p. 61: "A lethal dose..." "Zombies: When the Dead Walk."
*Enigma*, Season 4, Episode 7, directed by Donna Zuckerbrot, Gaiam, April 2008.

p. 58: "I was thirteen years old..." Philippe Charlier. *Zombies: An Anthropological Investigation of the Living
Dead.* Translated by Richard J. Gray II. University Press of Florida, 2015.

p. 60: The illustration is based on a photograph of Clairvius Narcisse taken by Jean-Claude Francolon in 1982.

p. 60: This paper presents the case studies of Wilfred D and MM: Roland Littlewood and Chavannes
Douyon. "Clinical findings in three cases of zombification." *The Lancet*, Vol. 350, October 11, 1997. p.
1094-1096. http://citeseerx.ist.psu.edu/viewdocdownload?doi=10.1.1.594.4233&rep=rep1&type=pdf

## Amazing Powers of the Mind

p. 60: "Ok, I'm getting something..." and all other Uri Geller quotes on this page come from "Dimbleby Talk-
In." BBC, November 23, 1973. http://www.urigeller.com/tv-radio/the-show-that-launched-uris-career/

p. 68: "It was running!!! ..." Charles Panati, Editor. *The Geller Papers.* Boston: Houghton Mifflin Company,
1976. p. 121.

p. 68: "I feel that these powers..." Uri Geller. *My Story.* New York: Praeger Publishers, 1975. p. 11.

p. 69: The story about Nina Kulagina comes from this book: Annie Jacobsen. *Phenomena: The Secret History
of the U.S. Government's Investigations into Extrasensory Perception and Psychokinesis.* New York: Little,
Brown, and Company, 2017.

p. 69: "We have observed..." Peter Gwynne. "Diets and Psychics." *New Scientist*, March 22, 1973. p. 676-677.

p. 71: Most of the ideas about how Geller may have used tricks in his performances come from: James
Randi. *The Truth About Uri Geller.* Prometheus Books, 1975.

p. 72: "Geller manipulates the experiments..." Joseph Hanlon. "Uri Geller and Science." *New Scientist*, October 17, 1974. p. 170-185.

p. 72: I'd like to thank psychologist Susan Blackmore for speaking with me about her early experiments into psychic phenomena that led her to the conclusion that these powers don't work. (She also once had tea with Uri Geller, who did not convince her he was a real psychic.)

p. 72: "I'm having a hard time..." and p. 77: "If you set people up..." Carl Charlson, Director. "Secrets of the Psychics" *Nova*, Season 20, Episode 12. https://www.youtube.com/watch?v=2MFAvH8m8aI

p. 73: "I noticed I was bending it..." and p. 74: "Our brain is..." Susana Martinez-Conde. Personal interview, August 16, 2018.

p. 74: "They are fooling themselves..." Christopher French. Personal interview, August 22, 2018.

p. 74–77: To learn more about how psychics and their clients work together to tell a story, see: Richard Wiseman. *Paranormality: Why we see what isn't there*. Spin Solutions Ltd, 2011.

## The Secrets of an Ancient Tomb

I'd like to thank Egyptologist Salima Ikram of the American University in Cairo for speaking with me about Egyptian beliefs.

p. 78: "It was a thrilling moment..." Howard Carter. "Tutankhamun: Anatomy of an Excavation. Howard Carter's diaries and journals. The first excavation season in the tomb of Tutankhamun. Part 1: October 28 to December 31, 1922." Oxford: Griffith Institute, 2010. http://www.griffith.ox.ac.uk/gri/4sea1not.html

p. 80: "As my eyes grew accustomed..." Carter, Howard and Arthur Cruttenden Mace. *The Discovery of the Tomb of Tutankhamen*. Mineola, NY: Dover Publications, 1977. p. 96.

p. 82: My main source on the history of the curse of King Tut, including Sir Arthur Conan Doyle's reaction: Roger Lockhurst. *The Mummy's Curse: The True History of a Dark Fantasy*. Oxford, UK: Oxford University Press, 2012.

p. 83: "Something dreadful..." "Carnarvon's Brother Dies: Death of Aubrey Herbert Revives Superstition on Pharaoh's Tomb." *The New York Times*, September 28, 1923. https://timesmachine.nytimes.com/timesmachine/1923/09/28/104968971.html?pageNumber=7

p. 83: "O all people who enter..." Hawass, Zahi. *The Valley of the Golden Mummies*. Cairo, Egypt: The American University in Cairo Press, 2000. p. 94-95.

p. 85: "It is certain that the Egyptians..." Rose Eveleth. "The Curse of the Unlucky Mummy." *Nautilus*, April 10, 2014. http://nautil.us/issue/12/feedback/the-curse-of-the-unlucky-mummy

p. 87: This is the study into the life expectancy of people exposed to mummies: Mark R. Nelson. "The mummy's curse: historical cohort study." *British Medical Journal*, December 21, 2002. p. 1482-1484. https://www.ncbi.nlm.nih.gov/pmc/articles/PMC139048/

p. 89: "Many people wish to see..." Xiuzhen Li. Personal interview, September 12, 2018.

## Lost at Sea

p. 90: "Cleared for takeoff" and other details surrounding the disappearance of MH370: "Why Planes Vanish." *NOVA*. Season 41, Episode 16, October 8, 2014.

p. 90: "Good night Malaysian..." *The Telegraph*. "MH370 latest: Pilot spoke final words from cockpit, says wife." June 24, 2014. https://www.telegraph.co.uk/news/worldnews/australiaandthepacific/australia/10921910/MH370-latest-Pilot-spoke-final-words-from-cockpit-says-wife.html

p. 91 The map illustration is based on: Sean O'Key and Rachel Clarke. "Mapping MH370: Takeoff, disappearance, searches ... and debris found." CNN, September 2, 2016. https://edition.cnn.com/2015/07/30/asia/mh370-maps-of-takeoff-disappearance-search/index.html

p. 93: "I don't know where we are..." and p. 94: "Some external cause..." and p. 98: "I'm sure I'm in the Keys..." and "If we would just fly west..." Kusche, Larry. *The Bermuda Triangle Mystery Solved*. New York: Gallahad Books, 2006. p. 104-105 and 108 and 137.

p. 94: "This relatively limited area..." Gaddis, Vincent H. "The Deadly Bermuda Triangle." *Argosy*, February 1964. p. 28-29. https://www.physics.smu.edu/pseudo/BermudaTriangle/vincentgaddis.txt

p. 94: Bruce Gernon tells his story in this book: Rob MacGregor and Bruce Gernon. *The Fog: A Never Before Published Theory of the Bermuda Triangle Phenomenon*. Woodbury, Minnesota: Llewellyn Publications, 2013.

p. 96: Here is the astrophysicist who investigated Gernon's story: James Webb. "The UFO Hunters Debacle." *CSI*, September 2009. October 11, 2018. https://www.csicop.org/sb/show/ufo_hunters_debacle

p. 96: Here is the astrophysicist's investigation of who investigated Gernon's story: James Webb. "The UFO Hunters Debacle." CSI, September 2009. October 11, 2018. https://www.csicop.org/sb/show/ufo_hunters_debacle

p. 99: "That big airplane..." and p. 100: "That person could have been..." John Goglia. Personal interview, September 24, 2018.

p. 100: My main source for the hypoxia theory was: Christine Negroni. *The Crash Detectives: Investigating the World's Most Mysterious Air Disasters*. Penguin Books, 2016.

## Chapter 9: The Mystery of Dead Mountain

The deceased hikers names were: Yuri Doroshenko, Lyudmila Dubinina, Igor Dyatlov, Alexander Kolevatov, Yuri Krivonischenko, Zinaida Kolmogorova, Rustem Slobodin, Nikolai Thibeaux-Brignolle, and Alexander Zolotarev.

p. 102: "I wonder what awaits us…" and "an unknown compelling force" and p. 105: "I can't tell for sure…" Donnie Eichar. *Dead Mountain*. San Francisco: Chronicle Books, 2013. p. 37 and 225 and 229.

p. 103: "It was just still, completely still…" Keith McCloskey. Personal interview, May 29, 2018.

p. 106: "According to recent reports…" Teodora Hadjiyska. "Now we know snowmen exist." Dyatlov Pass. https://dyatlovpass.com/controversy

p. 106: My main source for the history of yeti and bigfoot was: Michael McLeod. *Anatomy of a Beast: Obsession and Myth on the Trail of Bigfoot*. University of California Press, 2011.

p. 108: "seven feet tall…" and "pushed against the walls…" Fred Beck and Ronald A. Beck. "I Fought the Apemen of Mount St. Helens, WA." *The Bigfoot Classics*, 27 September 1967. http://www.bigfootencounters.com/classics/beck.htm

p. 108: "On two feet it resembles…" Kelly Grosfield. "Local Man Says He Found Bigfoot." *My Panhandle*, 14 September 2017. https://www.mypanhandle.com/news/local-man-says-he-found-bigfoot/811261583

p. 110: "Science doesn't reject…" Bryan Sykes. Personal interview, June 4, 2018.

p. 110: Charlotte Lindqvist, an evolutionary biologist and bear expert at State University of New York in Buffalo, has also analyzed DNA that supposedly came from Yeti and determined it came from bears.

p. 110: Bryan Sykes told me a story about following a Bigfoot hunter into the woods to investigate a strange knocking sound. The real source? The wind knocked hollow trees together.

p. 110: Donnie Eichar, author of Dead Mountain, first proposed the infrasound theory.

p. 111: The illustration depicts a photograph found on a camera that belonged to the hikers.

## Monsters of the Deep

p. 114: "round, flat, and full of arms…" and "take to their oars…" Erik Pontoppidan. *The Natural History of Norway*. A. Berthelson, translator. London: Printed for A. Linde, 1755. https://books.google.com/books?id=3OglUqRF_soC

p. 115: "Monstrous arms like trees…" Richard Boyle. "When the squid sank a schooner." *The Sunday Times*, December 12, 1999. http://www.sundaytimes.lk/991212/plus5.html

p. 116: The illustration is based on a famous photo of Nessie known as "The Surgeon's Photograph," because it was supposedly taken by the doctor Robert Kenneth Wilson.

p. 117: The illustration is based on Sandra Mansi's photo, available here: Robert E. Bartholomew. "New Information Surfaces On 'World's Best Lake Monster Photo,' Raising Questions." *Skeptical Inquirer*, Vol. 37, No. 3, May/June 2013. https://skepticalinquirer.org/2013/05/new_information_surfaces_on_worlds_best_lake_monster_photo_raising_question/

p. 117: "I could see that it was living." and "Suddenly, the lake demon arose…" Benjamin Radford and Joe Nickell. *Lake Monster Mysteries*. Lexington, Kentucky: The University Press of Kentucky, 2006. p. 55 and 123

p. 118: "Because of my own personal experience…" John Kirk. Personal interview, September 25, 2018.

p. 119: Find out about the Nessie photograph hoax here: Joe Nickell. "Nessie Hoax Redux." *CSI*, March 1996. https://www.csicop.org/sb/show/nessie_hoax_redux

p. 121: "I was now the possessor…" and other information on the history of sea monsters: Richard Ellis. *Monsters of the Sea*. New York: Alfred A. Knopf, 1994. p. 130-131.

p. 122: "It's a giant squid…" and "Oh!" and all other descriptions of the Triton's dives: "Monster Squid: The Giant is Real." *Curiosity* Season 2 Episode 13. Discovery Channel, January 27, 2013. DVD.

p. 122: "Opens up possibilities…" Edith Widder. Personal interview, October 1, 2018.

p. 123 The giant squid that Kubodera and his team filmed was missing its two long feeding tentacles.

## Acknowledgements

I'd like to thank all of the scholars, scientists, and individuals who contributed their time and expertise to assist me with the research for this book. The Center for Inquiry (centerforinquiry.org) and its Skeptical Inquirer magazine (skepticalinquirer.org) are excellent resources for anyone interested in investigating mysteries through the lens of science and reason.

Quarto
Knows

Inspiring | Educating | Creating | Entertaining

Brimming with creative inspiration, how-to projects, and useful information to enrich your everyday life, Quarto Knows is a favourite destination for those pursuing their interests and passions. Visit our site and dig deeper with our books into your area of interest: Quarto Creates, Quarto Cooks, Quarto Homes, Quarto Lives, Quarto Drives, Quarto Explores, Quarto Gifts, or Quarto Kids.

First published in 2019 by Frances Lincoln Children's Books, an imprint of The Quarto Group.
400 First Avenue North, Suite 400, Minneapolis, MN 55401, USA.
T (612) 344-8100 F (612) 344-8692 **www.QuartoKnows.com**

ISBN 978-1-78603-784-8
These artworks were painted with gouache and acrylic and put together digitally.
Set in Aller, Azaelia, and Kelpt

Published by Rachel Williams
Designed by Nicola Price
Edited by Katie Cotton
Production by Nicolas Zeifman

Manufactured in Guangzhou, China EB082020

3 5 7 9 8 6 4 2